Felling The Ancient Oaks

JOHN MARTIN ROBINSON

Felling The Ancient Oaks

How England Lost its Great Country Estates

Aurum
history

First published 2011 by
Aurum Press Limited
7 Greenland Street
London NW1 0ND
www.aurumpress.co.uk

ISBN 978 1 84513 670 3

10 9 8 7 6 5 4 3 2 1
2015 2014 2013 2012 2011 2010

Endpapers: *front* Trentham; *back* Deepdene.

p.1 photograph: Felling the timber on the Whilagh estate
(Getty Images)

p.2-3: Witley Court
(English Heritage/National Monuments Record)

p.4-5: Cassiobury
(English Heritage/National Monuments Record)

p.6-7: Haggerston Castle
(English Heritage/National Monuments Record)

Book design by Peter Ward

Printed and bound in Singapore

While you have fed upon my seignories,
Dispark'd my parks, and fell'd my forest-woods,
From mine own windows torn my household-coat,
Raz'd out my impress, leaving me no sign,
Save men's opinions, and my living blood,
To shew the world I am a gentleman.

Richard II, Act III
William Shakespeare (1597)

Contents

✿ Introduction ✿

'I'm sorry, but it's the horses, you know . . .' Owned by the Bassetts since the thirteenth century, Tehidy in Cornwall had been inherited by the 18-year-old Arthur Bassett in 1888. Thanks to tin mining, the 17,000-acre estate brought in £30,000 a year. But the bottom dropped out of tin, and this, combined with absurd extravagance and gambling, forced the sale of the estate to a London syndicate in 1916. The syndicate felled the timber and sold the house for a sanatorium, which burned down in 1919. The words quoted above are Bassett's apology to one of his tenant farmers. However, the role of racehorses in the decay of estates should perhaps be underlined for it was not just gambling: horse-breeding and racing were both expensive pastimes with a tendency to divert large resources away from economic estate development. Over the years much land has been sold to pay for horses. This underlines that individual character and weakness has played a role in the destiny of the English landed estate.

In the last one hundred years or so there has been a severe diminution in the number of English estates, with a third having disappeared and most reduced in size by 50 per cent or more since 1880. It is difficult to be precise from the available statistics, though. As ever, personal incompetence and extravagance, individual whim and the inevitable extinction of some old land owning families have all played a part in the ruin and extinction of property. But it has not just been the horses, amateur theatricals or poor judgement: what has undermined the great estates in the last century has been a result of social change and economic decline, capital taxation to pay for two destructive World Wars, occasional political hostility (especially on the part of radicals within the Liberal Party in the late nineteenth and early twentieth centuries), not to mention relentless urbanisation and uncontrolled over-population.

✿ *The Ionic portico at exterior of Witley Court designed by John Nash, and the exterior remodelled in Italian style by S. W. Dawkes. The house was gutted by fire in 1937 and the estate subsequently asset-stripped. The ruined shell survives in English Heritage guardianship.*

✿ *'Hermit' (The Marquess of Hastings' nemesis), the horse that won the Derby: the Marquess had put £100,000 on another horse which lost, the beginning of the end of the Donington estate.*

The country estate is one of England's most enduring picturesque images: a mellow country house surrounded by gardens, parkland, farms and woods with an attendant village or cottages, and a church with family tombs. This is the estate whose partial demise is chronicled here. It comprises large blocks of land in unified ownership (often complicated trusts but usually perceived as a single family). Professionally managed by land agents, lawyers and trustees as well as the owner himself, directing teams of farm managers, head foresters, surveyors with an eye to long-term conservation as well as immediate economic profit, it has thus proved an unusually effective way of preserving open landscape and historic buildings, managing farms, woods, coverts, hedges, rivers and water. An estate has always provided several attributes, not least income for its owner, but also administration, display, hospitality, sport, leisure and social prestige. Between the seventeenth and nineteenth centuries the ownership of a landed estate was also the basis of political power, when in England the landed aristocracy took over much of the role of government from the Crown, thus laying the foundations for late nineteenth- and early twentieth-century 'parliamentary democracy' and the bureaucratic managerial system which now controls those aspects of

English life not governed directly by the European Union.

The landed estate was an important part of the social, historical and topographical as well as the economic fabric of England. It explains why much of the English landscape looks as it does, for England is entirely a manmade landscape and not a wild one. Quite possibly, this is one of the principal reasons why proportionately it is better preserved and more beautiful to look at than many other developed countries despite the last three centuries of intense industrialisation, urbanisation and exponential population growth. The population, which was about 10 million in 1800, had reached over 40 million by 1900, 60 million in the course of the twentieth century and is heading for 70 million in the twenty-first century. By 2050, England is predicted to have the largest as well as the densest population in Europe. Despite this, much of the historic pattern and character of the landscape has survived and is likely to continue to some degree. Indeed, the English landed estates have played an important (and generally unacknowledged) modern role in protecting the English countryside.

When Green Belts, National Parks, Town and Country Planning, listed building legislation and overall state control of land-use were gradually introduced in the middle of the twentieth century, not to mention the often admirable conservation work of the National Trust, this achievement was built on the existing pattern of the landed estates. For instance, the new South Downs National Park in Sussex largely comprises 'unspoilt landscape', owned and preserved (though only 60 miles from central London) by the traditional management policies of the Petworth, Arundel, Cowdray, Goodwood, West Dean, Wiston, Parham and other historic estates in the area. Without those estates the land would have been built over and fragmented during the last 150 years. The Green Belt in North Surrey similarly follows a string of historic estates between Dorking and Guildford, including Albury, Shere, Polesden Lacey, Denbies, Hatchlands and Clandon, some of whose owners entered into voluntary covenants with each other after the First World War not to develop their land (or gave it to the National Trust), thus preserving much of the area which is now statutorily protected by the Metropolitan Green Belt.

The destruction of landed estates in England runs parallel to the twentieth-century destruction of the English country house and shares several of the same causes, although the parallel is not exact. On many occasions an estate survived when the principal house was demolished; on the other hand, the house itself has sometimes survived in institutional use like a stranded sea monster gasping for breath when the supporting land has been broken up and sold, or built over. Generally, a family tried to hang onto their land even when the upkeep of the big house seemed impossible. Some estates, especially in attractive rural areas, when sold have been bought by new owners keen to continue traditional country life. Even today, on the open market handsome estate landscape with traditional amenities including 'sporting' and a country house, especially in fashionable counties such as Shropshire or Wiltshire, remains more valuable than ordinary open farmland. But generally, especially in the old industrial and urban regions – South Lancashire, the Midlands, the West Riding and the South East – landed estates have disappeared under brick, tarmac and concrete, cut up by motorways and ring roads, built over by new towns and

⊗ *The Minister of Transport Ernest Marples admiring the M1 motorway which sliced through several Midlands estates and used the stone from Nuttall Temple for its foundations.*

⊗ *Derwent church spire stranded in a reservoir in Derbyshire. The whole estate heartland there disappeared under water.*

⊕ *Derwent Hall, Catholic chapel, formal gardens and landscape before the estate was flooded to make Ladybower Reservoir in the early twentieth century.*

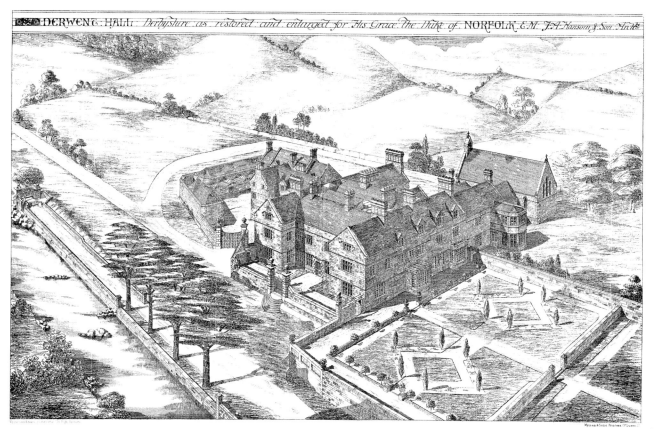

suburbs, airports, power stations and shacks for industry, retail and distribution, or flooded for reservoirs in the course of the twentieth century.

THE ORIGINS OF THE ESTATE

In the early Middle Ages an estate comprised wide areas of general jurisdiction as well as the demesne farm of the owner. An estate, or fief, was more an assemblage of customary rights and revenues than a physical unit. The Norman Conquest introduced to England the Frankish feudal system whereby land was held by service to the Crown, often military service although not necessarily so. This laid the foundations of the English estate as it developed over subsequent centuries and was partly responsible for the principle of primogeniture (inheritance by the eldest son or senior male heir), which has been the most distinctive and practically successful feature of hereditary English landowning. Originally a military necessity, the practice came to be more consistently developed in England than elsewhere and was responsible for several of the special characteristics of the landed estate, and indeed for its survival into the modern age rather than being dispersed and wasted among myriad heirs and rival siblings.

Over the centuries English estates have been held together by the consistent application of primogeniture, but very often this has involved descent to a sister's son or more remote relation rather than directly to a son of the owner as he either did not marry himself or did not produce a male heir of his own (this was part genetically preconditioned as a result of regularly marrying heiresses who *per se* tended to come from families with a low ability to produce boys). A great many English estates have therefore passed through the female line and a direct male-line descent of property from the early Middle Ages to modern times in England is very rare. This frequent

℘ *Petworth, Sussex. The classic great estate developed out of a medieval fief of the Percys, Earls of Northumberland. The park was landscaped by Capability Brown in the mid-eighteenth century. Beyond is the Stag Park turned into a model farm by the 3rd Earl of Egremont in the 1790s, and praised by Arthur Young: 'His Lordship's estates are conducted upon a great scale in the highest style of improvement'. Pioneering crops included rhubarb and the opium poppy grown for medicine, and the buildings a semi-circular hoggery. In the foreground can be seen solid 19th-century labourers' cottages and a generous provision of allotments typical of Victorian estate development.*

descent of estates through females is not immediately obvious because almost always the heir took the name and arms that went with the estate by Royal Licence, thus seeming to perpetuate the dynasty of the male line. On the whole, English landowners were 'terrilineal' – their surname went with their estate.

Prince Pückler-Muskau, the German visitor and commentator on Britain in the reign of George IV, was intrigued by the distinctive tradition of the English land-owning class: 'It dazzles only by the old historic names, so wisely retained, which appear through the whole of English history like standing masks; though new families often of very mean and even discreditable extraction are continually concealed behind them.'

A significant development in the late Middle Ages was the evolution of new legal arrangements to avoid partible inheritance and ensure a family's survival as a landed dynasty. This involved granting the property to trustees for a specific use – namely to keep the bulk of the property intact in the male line while making provision for widows for life and, to a less extent, for other members of the family. In the seventeenth century this developed into the 'strict entail', which settled an estate for three generations at a time on the senior male heir and was constantly renewed until the twentieth century when more tax-efficient, flexible trusts were devised.

There also developed sophisticated systems of administration with an official class of Receivers, Secretaries, Reeves and Bailiffs, Annual Audits and written records and accounts, chartularies and valors (estate inventories). By the fifteenth century, most Norman labour dues or manual service had been commuted to rents, nearly always paid in cash. Though faint remnants of old feudal dues and rights lingered on into the early twentieth century, most were abolished in the mid-seventeenth century.

As well as the development of systematised and centralised estate administration, there were also significant changes in practical estate economy (triggered by the loss of a third of the English population in the Black Death, from 1348–53). This reduction in the population led to a shortage of labour and higher wages (and therefore a higher standard of living for the remaining inhabitants). No longer were landowners able to till their large demesne farms with cheap, serf labour and there was a switch to a *rentier* economy, with much of the land divided up and leased out to tenants for cash rents. Thus the late-medieval countryside came to be made up of two types of property: 'copyhold' (the old long-term customary manorial tenures,

so-called because title was based on a copy of the manorial records) and land that was let on short leases to rent-paying tenants. Over time, copyhold gradually became freehold and the basis of the non-estate landscape, the tenanted land the nucleus of landed estates in modern times. The growth of sheep farming and wool production – the mainstay of the English economy during the fifteenth and sixteenth centuries – led to arable land being put down to pasture and enclosed with walls, hedges and fences, a process which continued in England until the early nineteenth century, by which time nearly all the lowland landscape including arable fields had been enclosed to create the unique and tidy jigsaw pattern of the English countryside with its rectangular hedged and walled fields. In the seventeenth and eighteenth centuries, enclosure and concentration of landholdings required individual Acts of Parliament, but this was speeded up at the end of the century by legislation enabling general enclosure on a parish basis by parliamentary commissioners who investigated all rights and ownerships and divided up the landscape accordingly, so that it could be enclosed as individual farms and smallholdings.

The Normans and Plantagenets can be credited with several distinctive features of the English estate, not least the exploitation of its sporting uses, the invention of the park and the introduction of fallow deer,[1] rabbits and organised hunting. Indeed, the deer park was the medieval status symbol *par excellence*. By the fourteenth century there were over 3,000 deer parks in England, some great landowners having several parks. As well as deer, they were stocked with other animals such as wild cattle. The famous herds of primeval white cattle at Chillingham Castle in Northumberland and Chartley Castle in Staffordshire represent survival of the latter. Rabbits were the other principal inhabitants of a medieval park and they were first imported to southeast England from the Continent *circa* 1200. At first they were housed in special warrens and protected, but soon they spread everywhere.

Medieval parks were always wooded as one of their functions was to provide timber as well as shelter for the deer, and this is the origin of the 'forest glade' character of parks with alternating woods and grass, which was perpetuated for aesthetic reasons in later centuries. In the eighteenth century, some medieval parks were transformed into landscape parks – for instance at Windsor, Beaudesert, Lathom, Lyme, Hatfield or Petworth.

1 Red deer and roe deer are native wild animals, as are foxes. Pheasants were introduced by the Romans while grouse are native.

Most existing English parks, however, were created from scratch at a later date but consciously reflect the venerable character of medieval parks and protecting old trees within their bounds, as with the Panshanger Oak within Repton's landscape of 1799 at Panshanger in Hertfordshire.

The sixteenth century saw a quickening of the market for land with the transfer to private hands of large tracts from the Church and Crown – perhaps a quarter of all the land in England in a century. The grant and sales of church and monastic land to private individuals had significant social and economic consequences, augmenting many existing landholdings and leading to the establishment of new estates which perpetuated the monastic names: Woburn Abbey, Combermere Abbey, Beaulieu Abbey, Lacock Abbey and Mottisfont Abbey, to name but a few which survive in private or National Trust ownership.

The Howard Dukes of Norfolk augmented their then large holdings in East Anglia with the estates of Castle Acre, Sibton, Croxton and Thetford Priories and the Grey Friars in Norwich, as well as the Charterhouse in London (none still in ducal hands, thanks to Elizabethan attainders for treason). The Manners, Earls of Rutland, acquired Rievaulx Abbey and Warter Priory in Yorkshire (later sold on to other owners), as well as monastic land adjoining their seat at Belvoir Castle in Leicestershire, which still forms part of that estate. The Earls of Shrewsbury also did conspicuously well, acquiring Worksop and Rufford in Nottinghamshire, Rotherham in Yorkshire and Glossop in Derbyshire.

As well as augmenting the holdings of the great owners, this dissemination of old church land swelled the ranks of the lesser landowners or gentry, often the descendants of lawyers or merchants newly investing in land and establishing themselves as country squires. The new patterns of ownership varied from county to county. In Essex, Hertfordshire and Bedfordshire, for example, the proximity of London led to an influx of courtiers, royal servants and administrators who established themselves as new landowners on the strength of the profits of office. The estate landscape of Hertfordshire, for instance, is essentially a sixteenth-century creation. Most of the western half of the county had belonged to the abbey of St Albans until the 1540s. Eleven former monasteries were converted into houses after the demolition of their churches, including Ashridge, Cassiobury, Hitchin and Royston. All went in the twentieth century, though the park at Ashridge was a National Trust purchase in the 1920s. In remoter areas such as South Wales, Somerset and Gloucestershire the land went to merchants from Bristol whereas in the Midlands the abbey estates passed mainly to existing landowners,

such as the Rutlands, Shrewsburys, Heneages, Willoughbys and Berties, all of whom to a greater or lesser extent are still landed, as well as to merchants like the Levesons at Trentham and lawyers who were ubiquitous purchasers of land in the sixteenth century – new fortunes, then as now, being possible from a legal career.

The fluid land market continued under the Stuarts in the seventeenth century, with the large-scale sales and dispersal of Crown lands, often to public servants, before as well as during the Commonwealth. Even Windsor Great Park was sold during the Commonwealth (Charles II had to buy it back at the Restoration). Thomas Sackville, 1st Earl of Dorset, was typical – as Lord Treasurer to James I, he sold himself the Knole estate in Kent at a knockdown price. The rise of the Cecils is the classic example of a family who made good out of the largesse of the Crown. Robert Cecil, 1st Earl of Salisbury, inherited Theobalds in Hertfordshire and a house in Chelsea from his father, Queen Elizabeth's principal minister, the great Lord Burghley. Between 1598 and his death in 1612, he built up an entirely new landed estate, however. He sold the Chelsea house and bought and developed a larger property in St Martin's Lane. In addition, he speculated in Crown land and the confiscated estates of attainted noblemen, buying and selling property for profit. He bought the Cranborne estate in Dorset from the Crown and consolidated that estate with further grants and purchases, whereupon he built a charming hunting lodge at Cranborne Manor, near the site of an old royal castle. In 1607, he transferred his father's house at Theobalds to James I and in return was granted Hatfield (a former church property) by the King, where he built a large new house and rounded off the estate by buying the rectory, woods, freeholds, copyholds and most of the town. The majority of Robert Cecil's land was Crown land bought with the profits of his various court offices. Today, the whole of this early seventeenth-century land holding survives in the hands of his direct male descendant, Robert Cecil, present Marquess of Salisbury, and this represents a remarkable continuous achievement, even in England.

The Civil War in the middle of the seventeenth century had a serious impact on English estates, with much destruction and general damage to property, felling of timber and fines for being on the wrong side. Indeed, it cost the 2nd Earl of Salisbury £30,000 in arrears of rent and damage to his property, including the ransacking of Cranborne Manor. Much of the economic dislocation and damage was short-term, though several landowners lost part or all of their estates for ever, including the Earls of Derby, many of whose lands were never restored. The

10th Earl commemorated this ingratitude of Charles II in a remarkable inscription on the new Palladian portico at Knowsley, built in 1732:

> James Earl of Derby, Lord of Man and the Isles, Grandson of James Earl of Derby and of Charlotte, Daughter of Claude Duke of Tremouille whose husband James was beheaded at Bolton, XV October 1654, for strenuously adhering to King Charles II, who refused a bill unanimously passed by both Houses of Parliament for restoring to the family the estates which he lost by his loyalty to him. 1732.

The situation was generally saved after the Restoration by more entrepreneurial management of estates, the draining of fens and agricultural improvements, including new crops, planting of woods and new rental systems, as well as converting remaining manorial copyholds to leaseholds or enfranchising them for cash. In addition, English farming was consistently profitable from 1670 until the late nineteenth century, a period of 200 years of rising landed prosperity.

Thus by the beginning of the eighteenth century the English estate was ready for the 'age of improvement'. This was to be the most enterprising phase in the history of English farming and landscape with new agricultural theories, scientific improvements to crops and livestock, plus the introduction of planned, regular rotations. It culminated in the late eighteenth and early nineteenth century when the Board of Agriculture was founded by William Pitt's government and promulgated modern land-management and farming policies. Arthur Young, Secretary to the Board of Agriculture, published his agricultural tours of English counties, describing English estates at that time. The Holkham and Woburn sheep-shearings were instituted in the same years as the forerunners of the Royal Agricultural Show, with exhibitions of farmstock, new techniques and machinery. Many landowners, not least King George III himself at Windsor, were personally engaged in farming on their estates and took a keen personal interest in the management and improvement of their property. At Windsor, George III had two large model farms: the Norfolk and Flemish Farms, each with a different system of farming and crop rotation as a demonstration for English farmers in general.

English farming and the activities of English landowners were the wonder and envy of Europe, as well as a constant source of remark by foreigners: French, Russians, Swiss, Germans and Americans. George Washington kept up a regular correspondence with officials of the British Board of Agriculture and enterprising Britons such as Sir John Sinclair, a leading 'improver'. François de la Rochefoucauld was sent by his father to study English estates and farming in Suffolk. Catherine the Great was so impressed by English estate management that she set up a college in the grounds of Tsarskoe Selo in Russia to teach English methods and employed Samuel Bentham (brother of Jeremy Bentham, the utilitarian theorist) to advise on the development of farms and villages in the newly conquered Crimean provinces. Meanwhile, the Swiss published an encyclopaedia devoted to English agriculture, *La Bibliothèque Britannique*.

THE EIGHTEENTH-CENTURY ESTATE

The development of the English (and Scottish) estate in the eighteenth century was a product of the Enlightenment and is a fascinating reflection of contemporary socio-economic, artistic and scientific ideals and theories. The distinctive English aesthetic – the Picturesque – emerged out of the eighteenth-century landowner's way of looking at his estate and his plans for improving it in the manner of landscape painting. Utilitarianism, neo-Classicism, science, Romanticism, Moral Humanitarianism, the cult of the simple life ... many of the important eighteenth-century intellectual concerns were reflected in estate management and given permanent form by agricultural and landscape improvement.

It was a reflection of the long-lasting English love of rural life, and indeed the special attraction exerted by the land on the educated eighteenth-century Englishman was further enhanced by his classical schooling and Grand Tour: Virgil's, Horace's and even Cicero's writings overflow with praise of rural life. The landowner viewed himself as a latter-day Roman, the inheritor of all the classical literary resonances pervading agricultural and rural life; he saw his house, park and farms as a recreation of Pliny's villa at Tusculum, Horace at Tivoli or Virgil's *Georgics*.

The improvement of an estate was also considered a patriotic duty. Eighteenth-century economic theorists emphasised agriculture was the foundation of a prosperous and well-populated state: improvements therefore helped to strengthen England's economic and political position vis à vis her Continental rivals, especially France. Good farming fed a growing urban and manufacturing nation; well-managed woodland provided timber for the ships of the Royal Navy, the bulwark of Britain's status as a great power.

As well as new methods of arable farming and stock breeding plus the introduction of new crops, the eighteenth century also witnessed the rationalisation and enlargement of landholdings as owners bought adjoining property, sometimes selling outlying land elsewhere, in order to create more manageable, compact, unified and practical properties. Some estates amalgamated several smaller properties, as at Panshanger in Hertfordshire, where successive Georgian Earls Cowper were brought together by the purchase of four different smaller estates (rich landowners bought up their poorer neighbours). This expansion and consolidation of estates led to the reorganisation and amalgamation of farms, construction of new roads and bridges, new farm buildings, new plantations, new houses, new cottages, even new villages. Very large sums were invested. Coke of Norfolk, the most admired landowner of the age, claimed to have spent half a million pounds in his lifetime on improvements at Holkham, Norfolk. Prudent landowners ploughed at least a proportion of their income back into estate improvements and vied with each other in the scale and sophistication of new buildings and other works.

The rapid economic development of estates in the eighteenth century, the agglomeration of land and advances in agriculture led to the emergence of a new professional class, men who specialised in the management of land and property: the 'land agent' ('agent' in this sense being an eighteenth-century English usage). The emergence of the professional land agent operating out of a purpose-built office created a system of centralised management by professionals who specialised in the day-to-day administration and supervision of tenants, rents, leases and agreements, the maintenance of buildings and landscape. It is the good management of these men which was responsible over a 200-year period for the distinctive, well-kept look of the traditional estate that marks it out from ill-kempt, patchy, often treeless and ugly non-estate landscape.

Such agents were sometimes 'gentlemen of the second class' or army officers, while others came from Scottish farming families noted in the eighteenth and nineteenth centuries for their special expertise; Edinburgh University being the first in Britain with an agricultural faculty in the late eighteenth century. Francis Blaikie, Coke of Norfolk's agent at Holkham, was an example of the new Scottish expert in land-management, as was James Loch, the Duke of Sutherland's Edinburgh-educated agent-in-chief, who planned the controversial early nineteenth-century Enlightenment improvements on the Trentham and Lilleshall estates in Staffordshire and Shropshire, as well as in the Highlands of Scotland. Some families, like

the Wyatts – originally farmers, builders and surveyors in Staffordshire – produced a whole dynasty of land agents in the late eighteenth and early nineteenth centuries. Indeed, the Wyatts established themselves as resident agents for two or three generations at several estates, including Beaudesert and Shugborough in Staffordshire, Penrhyn in North Wales, Badminton in Gloucestershire and Croxteth in Lancashire. The Matthew Ellisons, a father-and-son team who managed the Duke of Norfolk's northern estates for nearly the whole of the nineteenth century and were largely responsible for the industrial development of Glossop and Sheffield, were another example of a brilliant, hereditary family of land agents.

The agricultural theorist Nathaniel Kent set up one of the first firms of specialist London estate agents, who for a standard scale of fees supervised estates for their owners and provided special advice or strategic reports on request. They were the forerunners of the big London property firms such as Cluttons, Smiths Gore, Knight Frank & Rutley or Savills in the nineteenth and twentieth centuries.

Many estates established purpose-built estate offices in the late eighteenth century. Arthur Young in his *General View of Lincolnshire* described as a model that belonging to Sir Joseph Banks at Revesby in Lincolnshire, which had two main rooms divided by a brick wall and with an iron door as a safeguard against fire. Furniture included map tables, bookcases, desks, levels and other surveying equipment, and a chest of drawers or filing cabinet numbered with a comprehensive index of names and subjects. The 11th Duke of Norfolk's Estate Office, Tower House at Arundel (built in 1790), continued in use for almost 200 years.

Under the agent and the Estate Office, the estate was divided into separate departments: building yard, woods, stables and kennels, game, home farm and dairy, gardens, each managed by a specialist: the clerk of works, the head forester, the head keeper, the farm manager and the head gardener. This sophisticated, skilled and competent management class oversaw the economic success of the late eighteenth- and nineteenth-century English estate, which increased production, feeding the growing urban population during the Napoleonic Wars and beyond (between 1790 and 1815, the land under cultivation in England was expanded to its widest extent since the Black Death and before the Second World War), while also enhancing its beauty with large-scale tree planting and picturesque landscape improvements.

The economic success of the Georgian estate was combined with aesthetic improvements that transformed

the appearance of the English landscape. Re-afforestation of England, following extensive clear-felling in the sixteenth and early seventeenth centuries, especially during the Civil War, began after the Restoration with the advocacy of the newly founded Royal Society and the diarist John Evelyn, whose book *Sylva: A Discourse of Forest Trees* (1664) was intended, as he put it in his dedication to Charles II, to encourage 'furnishing your almost exhausted Dominions with more than two million of timber trees'. This influential and popular book went through further editions in Evelyn's lifetime (in 1670 and 1679) and has remained in print ever since. Timber was necessary for the Navy, manufactures and building, but Evelyn urged a massive tree-planting programme not just for utility and profit but also for aesthetic reasons because trees and woods were the means of creating an ideal landscape. In the

course of the late seventeenth, eighteenth and nineteenth centuries the English estate was indeed so transformed.

In its early phases this meant a Franco-Dutch formal landscape with avenues, long straight rides, symmetrical terraces, geometrical layouts and canalised ponds. It is recorded in Kip and Knyff's engravings published in *Britannia Illustrata* or *Les Delices de la Grande Bretagne* in 1707. The Duke of Montagu's French-inspired late seventeenth-

Castle Howard, Yorkshire, a baroque palace in a monumental classical landscape which covers 12 square miles of farmland, woods, lakes, avenues and architectural outworks.

century system of avenues and formal woodland covered the whole estate at Boughton in Northamptonshire and still survives, currently being restored by the Duke of Buccleuch. Even more extensive was the massive planting scheme of the 1st Duke of Beaufort at Badminton, Gloucestershire, which radiated not just across his own land but far into the landscape beyond, where friendly (and deferential) neighbours cut their hedges and planted trees as a continuation of his lines and patterns. Today, they still underlie the landscape of South Gloucestershire.

Many of the trees used in these ambitious late seventeenth- and eighteenth-century estate planting programmes were imported as acorns, cones, seeds and saplings. Oaks came from the Mediterranean countries and from across the Atlantic; pines were from Corsica, Canada, Georgia and New England; firs and spruce from Scandinavia and North America. In the course of three centuries a vast quantity of trees, new species and shrubs were imported into England and planted on estates by their landowners. Larch and rhododendrons were first introduced into England in the mid-eighteenth century, greatly enriching estate woods and gardens. In 1766, the 1st Lord Scarsdale planted 'a rare Italian shrub rododendrone' in the park at Kedleston. Despised as *ponticum*, these incunabula rhododendrons have all been chopped down by the National Trust since it took over. The earliest larches in Britain were planted at Blair Atholl, Perthshire by the 7th Duke of Atholl, who fired the seeds out of a cannon at the hillsides in 1785.

THE LANDSCAPE GARDEN

Of course the most significant development in the story of eighteenth-century planting and improvement was the rise of the English landscape garden. The creation of philosophers, writers and *virtuosi*, inspired by poetry, classical landscape painting and foreign travel (especially to Italy), the English landscape garden was an original work of art. Landowners attempted to mould their properties to form pictures. As the writer Joseph Addison put it: 'a man might make a pretty landscape of his own possessions.'

The idea of planting a whole estate to resemble one natural landscape painting, to form beautiful prospects when viewed from the house or its grounds, or considered vantage points in the locality, was made possible by the invention of the sunken fence by the royal gardener Charles Bridgeman in his influential landscape layout at Stowe, Buckinghamshire, *circa* 1720.

The landscape at Castle Howard is the perfect example of the heroic age of English classical design, covering an area of 31 sq km (12 sq miles). Between the gardens and the surrounding farms there were no enclosing walls, so that 'all the country be laid open to view' and 'woods and fields and distant enclosures should have the care of the industrious planter,' as Addison advised. Castellated walls, obelisks, pyramids, temples, statues of Roman gods and heroes as well as a sublime domed mausoleum enriched the landscape.

> *If to Perfection these plantations rise*
> *If they agreeably my heirs surprise*
> *This faithful pillar will their age declare*
> *As long as Time these characters shall spare*
> *Here then with kind remembrance read his name*
> *Who for posterity perform'd the same*
> *Charles the III Earl of Carlisle*
> *of the family of the Howards*
> *Erected a castle where the old castle of Henderskelfe*
>   *stood and called it Castle Howard*
> *He likewise made the plantations in this park*
> *And all the out-works monuments and other*
> *Plantations belonging to the said seat.*
> *He began these works in the year MDCCCII*
> ANNO DM MDCCXXXI

So wrote Lord Carlisle on the tall stone obelisk of 1731 at the junction of his cross of avenues, thus underlining his motives. Fifty years later, Horace Walpole famously described the maturing results: 'Nobody had informed me that at one view I should see a palace, a town, a fortified city, temples on high places, woods worthy of being each a metropolis of the Druids, the noblest lawn in the world fenced by half the horizon, and a mausoleum that would tempt one to be buried alive . . .' The same idealistic outlook as that of the Earl of Carlisle is experienced a century later in the inscription on the Earl of Shrewsbury's Grecian monument at Alton Towers, Staffordshire, that Picturesque Elysium in the Churnet valley on the edge of the moors: 'He made the desert smile.' Indeed, one onlooker was surprised he hadn't been able to make it laugh aloud.

B Stourhead, Wiltshire, the ideal Augustan landscape. Georgian landowners followed the advice of Joseph Addison that 'a man might make a pretty landscape of his own possessions.'

✣ *The Glossop estate in Derbyshire was sold off in 1925. Glossop Hall is now an estate of bungalows nicknamed 'Noddy Town'.*

As developed by William Shenstone and William Kent in the 1730s, the English landscape movement took the country by storm. Some eighteenth-century layouts were the product of their owner's own taste and enthusiasm but many were the work of professional landscape designers, of whom 'Capability' Brown (1716–83) was the most famous. A contractor as well as a designer, he himself supervised the damming of lakes, planting of shelter belts and clumps plus the levelling and moving of earth, thereby making a fortune. In the process he inspired a whole school of competent eighteenth-century landscape designers: Thomas White, Richard Woods, John Webb and William Emes, who worked all over the country. Brown himself was a great artist and his parks at Blenheim, Chatsworth, Petworth and Bowood are superb creations and works of art as perfect as any painting.

The most famous landscape designer of the generation after 'Capability' Brown was the equally influential Humphry Repton (1752–1818), whose manner was popularised by his famous published *Observations on Landscape Gardening* and the unpublished 'Red Books', which showed the appearance of an estate before and after 'improvement' by means of moveable flaps. Repton's manner was richer and more intricate, less classically

arcadian than Brown's, more densely wooded, more 'inhabited' and ornamental, with thatched cottages and decorative buildings as well as 'useful' structures.

Architectural incidents in the form of Gothic ruins and towers or classical temples and belvederes, statues, obelisks, pyramids, columns and urns were all essential adjuncts of the designed landscape, forming eye-catchers and view-stoppers or memento mori. Not all Georgian estate architecture was merely decorative – quite the contrary. Much eighteenth- and nineteenth-century estate building took the form of model farms and cottages as writers and theorists stressed well-designed farm buildings were an important aspect of estate management. Coke of Norfolk's buildings in the large park and surrounding estate at Holkham were entirely practical: barns, farms, lodges and cottages for tenants, all designed by London architect Samuel Wyatt (1737–1807) in an appropriately austere neo-Classical manner and among the most original and progressive architecture of their date in Europe. Wyatt designed farm buildings at several other estates too, including Shugborough and Sandon in Staffordshire, Doddington in Cheshire, Somerley in Hampshire and Thorndon, Essex. Local architects and builders also specialised in providing new estate buildings, often to specialist plans laid down by the client's agent or the Board of Agriculture's expert theorists. The many new farm buildings and new houses and cottages built on the Trentham estate in Stafford-shire in the early nineteenth century were planned in detail by agent-in-chief James Loch and designed and built by estate architect John Smith and his successor, William Links.

The Georgian improvement of the landscape was not simply motivated by agricultural progress and a desire for visual enhancement, but also through the need to create and maintain habitats for game and field sports. Sport had been an essential feature of the country estate since the Normans, with their deer parks and hunting forests. This was still much the case in the eighteenth and nineteenth centuries with the development of new formalised types of hunting and shooting: fox hunting and driven game shooting. The improvement of the landscape for sporting purposes, particularly by the planting of trees for game coverts, careful control of natural vegetation and flora such as heather or the management of water, is responsible for many of the most distinctive features of the English landed estate and open landscape. Fox hunting largely superseded stag hunting in the middle of the eighteenth century, being more compatible with arable farming and the hedges of the enclosed landscape. Shoots with driven game and better guns first superseded the old walk-up methods at Holkham in the 1790s, where Coke of Norfolk was a pioneer in this, as in other fields of estate management. Many estates had their own packs of hounds and handsome architectural kennels are characteristic Georgian and Victorian estate buildings (at Milton in Northamptonshire they take the form of a ruined castle). At Goodwood (Sussex) and Brocklesby (Lincolnshire), James Wyatt designed splendid neo-Classical complexes where the hounds enjoyed such amenities as central heating and Grecian pediments.

Even more magnificent were Georgian stable blocks housing horses for hunting as well as riding, and also carriages. Often with handsome symmetrical elevations and clock turrets, they can be greater works of architecture than the house itself. In the twentieth century several were converted into the main house on the estate when the principal house was demolished. Many practically minded eighteenth-century architects, like Carr of York, specialised in the design of stable blocks. The stable buildings on Georgian estates were frequently among the most original and exciting English Palladian designs, as at Castle Howard, Woburn Abbey or Wentworth Woodhouse. James Paine's magnificent stable block at Chatsworth, deploying five different types of rustication and life-size stone stags in the carved Devonshire arms, is one of the finest examples of Georgian estate buildings.

THE VICTORIAN ESTATE

The Victorian age saw the heyday of the large landed estate with huge staffs, private cricket grounds, jollifications to celebrate local and national events, as well as the building of model cottages, new schools, new or restored churches and superb mechanised farm buildings. In retrospect, the Victorian estate seems to capture the best of both worlds, combining the mature visual results of Georgian Augustan improvement with the philanthropic and humanitarian achievements and technical progress of the nineteenth century.

The developments of the previous century now came to fruition as trees and landscapes matured and sporting became formalised with seasons for hunting, shooting and fishing. However, the High-Victorian estate did not differ from the late-Georgian estate in significant ways and was largely the product of developments in the previous century. Estates continued to expand up to the 1850s with

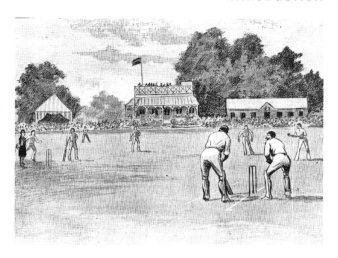

⚓ *The private cricket ground of the Earl of Sheffield at Sheffield Park, Sussex. The elaborate Victorian pavilion has been demolished. Many Victorian estates had their own fields.*

agricultural production and revenues doubling between 1820 and 1850. Improvement of the land combined with under-draining of fields, new artificial fertilisers such as guano from South America, new and bigger farm steadings, cottages and houses. Great Victorian landowners invested staggering amounts in new estate buildings, so continuing the Georgian tradition: £700,000 at Holkham, £832,274 at Woburn and £992,000 at Alnwick. Steam power was adopted for threshing machines and sawmills, with many solidly built Victorian industrial-scale farm buildings erected to make the most of technological advances. Farming continued to thrive and expand into the 1860s and 70s to feed the rapidly growing industrial and urban population of Britain. This was not the case in Ireland, however, where the population was reduced by half after the 1840s in the most dramatic incidence of voluntary birth control in modern history following the Famine, to make it sustainable without potatoes.

Victorian landowners were active church builders or restorers of old churches on their estates and this was their most distinctive architectural contribution to the English landed estate. Even those who were not strongly religious felt it incumbent on themselves to support the local parish as a social duty. In some areas, such as the North and East Ridings of Yorkshire, neighbouring landowners like the Franklands, Dawneys, Hothams and Sykeses vied with each other in the magnificence of their rebuilt churches. Those spires and towers still dominate the wide rolling landscape of the Wolds in an enduring monument to Victorian piety and philanthropy. This reflected the transformation of the ideal landowner from an Augustan 'man of taste' whose sensibilities were formed by the Grand Tour into the

'Christian gentleman' moulded by Dr Arnold's reformed public schools and Tractarian Oxford. Such people saw Christian philanthropy as part of their duty and built schools, reading rooms, working men's clubs, almshouses and other charitable institutions on their estates; they also created allotments so that all cottagers could grow vegetables. Above all, they built improved, ventilated, solid model dwellings for labourers. The peak of estate cottage building was between 1850 and 1870 when many estates built or renovated hundreds of cottages, which remain the best-built and most solid rural housing in Britain.

The staffing of a large estate in the nineteenth century was much the same throughout the country. Lyme Park in the bleak foothills of the Peak District, for instance, had a similar estate hierarchy and population to that of Holkham in Norfolk's rich arable lands. The building yard employed a blacksmith, plumbers, joiners, housepainters, wheelwright, drainers, wallers, labourers, roadmen and workshopmen, all under a clerk of works and a foreman. At Arundel, the building yard employed 100 labourers in the late nineteenth century and this was standard for a large estate. The game department at Lyme comprised a head keeper and five under-keepers, each responsible for one of the five drives of the pheasant shoot; there was also a kennel lad and a park keeper to look after the deer. Eight men were employed in the stables. The home farm establishment comprised a bailiff, shepherd, carter, cowmen, teamsmen and a poultry rearer. The head gardener, too, directed a large team, including an outside foreman and men to stoke the greenhouse boilers, as well as gardeners and boys. Most Victorian estates also had a brewhouse and laundry with their own staff.

With the household staff, the estate employees formed self-contained communities with their own parties and celebrations related to the year or events in the landowning family, such as coming-of-ages and marriage-homecomings, which were celebrated in the nineteenth century with revived medieval pageantry. Recreational facilities for the staff were developed on many Victorian estates. Most had cricket pitches while some had bowling greens and golf courses, as at Holkham or Chatsworth. Many estates had social clubs, where cocoa was served rather than ale. Billiards, dominoes, newspapers and books could also be enjoyed – it was all part of earnest Victorian attempts at social improvement and to mitigate the perceived evils of 'drink'. Temperance played a strong part in late-Victorian philanthropy, with the closing of alehouses. Non-alcohol serving social clubs were built in the villages at Sandringham in Norfolk, Castle Howard and

at Trentham, where there was only one inn on the estate and that was more a hotel than a pub, as was also the case at Holkham. The establishments on smaller estates were reduced versions of larger ones, with more compact workshops and fewer outbuildings, but a similar pattern of employment and possibly more pubs. Grander Whiggish estates were most teetotal and generally Tory estate villages had a pub with the family heraldry on a signboard: The Worsley Arms, The Assheton Arms, The Hoghton Arms.

The English estate at its most extensive in the 1860s was an economic entity that perfectly combined profitable farming with sport, social concerns, fine architecture and superb picturesque landscaping. It was uniquely successful in modern economic development in its synthesis of high culture, humane social concerns and commercial aims. Its owners, who were well-educated, took the lead in local life as lord lieutenants, high sheriffs, justices of the peace and patrons of charities. The estate was the backdrop to this practical and ceremonial activity.

The physical make-up of the high-Victorian estate comprised a series of large, well-arranged tenant farms with under-drained, neatly hedged fields and excellent solid masonry buildings – all producing high-quality food for the home market and export – interspersed with managed woodland and amenity tree planting: mature hedgerow timber, sporting coverts, shelter belts and mixed forestry. This type of planting is unique to British estates and in the 1860s much of it was one hundred years old and looked its mature best.

The focus of the estate was the estate village – large estates had several – with model cottages for the workforce: farm labourers, builders, craftsmen, foresters, keepers and roadmen. These were often overtly picturesque in architectural character. There were also some larger residences for the professionals: rector, agent, doctor and heads of estate departments. Allotments were available for growing vegetables or keeping a pig or a cow. The Norfolk estate in Sheffield in the 1780s was the first to provide allotments of this type and by the 1860s they were a standard provision on English estates so that tenants had their own fresh food.

The school was an important feature and there was also a reading room, social club, bowling green, shop, post office, inn (where the ethos was not temperance) or hotel and of course, a magnificent church (containing the tombs and memorials of the squirarchial family), which played a large role in the life of the community. It would have been restored to full Gothic glory at the height of the Tractarian

Movement in the 1850s and 60s by a leading architect of the time. Practical Christianity underpinned the whole system.

Impressive lodge gates formed an overture to the architecture of the 'big house'. Situated in a large, beautiful park and scrupulously maintained pleasure grounds, a large nineteenth-century country house was a community itself with acres of outbuildings: stables, kennels, laundry, brewhouse, workshops, building yard, sawmill, ice house, walled kitchen garden with extensive glasshouses, dairy, gas works, water pumping house, riding school, real tennis or squash court, possibly an aviary, even a private zoo (as at Knowsley, Woburn and Haggerstone). Country-house parks were also regularly used for military camps, reviews and training, so many had drill halls and rifle ranges. At its best, the Victorian estate system was an expression of contemporary social and practical concerns, with good primary education, some degree of healthcare and increasingly, old age pensions. Wages on a country estate were lower than in manufacturing towns – on average, 10/6 (52½p in today's money) a week – but housing was free and the estate paid the rates. Senior employees and keepers were provided with new suits once a year, cottagers with cloth to make their own as well as free fuel, water supply and similar facilities. Wages were supplemented with regular gifts of food and money, especially at Christmas (tea, sides of beef, oranges) or when ill (flannel underclothes and calves' foot jelly). Small monetary bequests to all employees on the death of the squire were an established Victorian tradition, too.

The main point is that an estate landscape provided

⚓ *Workington Hall, Cumberland. Under its eighteenth-century owner, John Christian Curwen, the Workington estate was the vanguard of agricultural improvement, noted for its model farm at the Schoose, prize-winning cultivation of carrots, and large-scale tree planting. Curwen's descendants were unwise enough to give this historic property to the town of Workington in the 1930s. The Council left it to rot and finally demolished most of the house in the 1960s including all the beautiful rooms designed by Carr of York. The Schoose is now a bleak caravan camp. Workington is one of the most depressed – and depressing towns – in England, a fate not unconnected with the dissolution of the Curwen estate.*

beauty for all who lived and worked there, or visited. The Victorians perpetuated the picturesque aesthetics of the Georgian era by careful professional management. Estate landscape is one of the great cultural achievements of the English. In the 1860s, they were at their most refulgent.

DEPRESSION AND DECLINE

This paternalist idyll, which must have seemed eternal in 1870, was no sooner achieved than shattered by the great agricultural depression that administered a severe blow to the economic foundations of the Victorian estate in the last decades of the nineteenth century. Indeed, it proved to be the harbinger of the insoluble financial problems that in the course of the twentieth century toppled Britain from world economic dominance. The reasons for changes in ownership and the break-up of historic estates are numerous and complex; they also vary from property to property. Incompetence, fecklessness and bad management on the part of owners have always played a part. The early nineteenth century had seen some spectacular collapses of estates. Wansted in Essex crashed in the 1820s, all its contents were sold in 1824 and the house – one of the finest Palladian structures in England, the work of Colin Campbell and the inspiration for the west front of Wentworth Woodhouse – was demolished to the ground. It was the result of uncontrolled expenditure and extravagance on the part of Wellesley Pole, who had married the Tilney heiress and gone through the whole of her large fortune in 20 years.

At Fonthill in Wiltshire, the notorious, reclusive millionaire William Beckford splurged the whole of his enormous Caribbean fortune derived from slaves and sugar on art and architecture, demolished his father's house, built Wyatt's Abbey (which collapsed because of inadequate foundations) and finally, to make ends meet sold his estates in Wiltshire and Somerset. The 3rd and 4th Lords Foley of Witley Court in Worcestershire squandered all their father's inheritance on general extravagance and gambling, then sold off the family's Worcestershire estate in 1833 (when the 4th Lord Foley married Lady Mary Fitzalan Howard his marriage settlement was burdened with £200,000 of debt). Then, in 1848, the Duke of Buckingham at Stowe went spectacularly bankrupt, selling the contents of the house and the majority of his estates. But these had been isolated examples. From 1880 on, the landowners rather than creating the waves suddenly found themselves in danger of being overwhelmed by strange tides and eddies from elsewhere.

The series of agricultural depressions between 1870 and 1896 after 30 years of constant prosperity (and 200 years of generally rising farm and rental income) naturally came as a great shock, especially in arable parts of England. What had at first seemed a temporary blip proved to be permanent, just like the twentieth-century collapse of manufacturing and other sectors of the British economy. Victorian England was a Free Trade country with a largely urban population and subsequent to the abolition of the Corn Laws in 1848 there was no tariff protection for homegrown produce. English farmers and landowners had to compete on the world market. Following the opening-up of the North American grain-growing West by railways and fast steam ships, it was cheaper to import grain than grow it at home. The invention of refrigerated ships made the same possible for meat, sheep from Australia and New Zealand, beef from Argentina, even eggs from China.

Unprotected English farming was ruined. Tenant farmers went bankrupt and gave up their holdings. Land proved difficult to re-let, even at greatly reduced rents. Landowners were forced to grant substantial rebates just to prevent the land (in which so much money had been invested) going derelict. The depression saw a severe decline in rentals, with many estate incomes dropping by half or two thirds between 1872 and the 1890s. Where landowners had large mortgages (and people had borrowed from the bank to buy land or improve their estates in the boom years), they now had to sell land and property to clear their debts or meet interest payments. In 1882, Parliament passed the Settled Land Act, which made it easier for landowners to sell entailed land. In retrospect, this marked the beginning of the dissolution of English estates. The decline in farming prosperity had a knock-on effect on land values, too. In 1871, before the agricultural crash, farmland had sold for £53 per acre but by the 1920s and 30s, the price had fallen to as low as £28 or even £23 per acre. This, in addition to the decline in income, made it less attractive for landowners to own 'surplus land'.

As has always been the case, the greater landowners with their wider geographical spread and range of investments, on the whole fared better than the smaller ones. It was the latter – who could not generally subsidise their estate from urban property, ground rents, mineral royalties or shares in South American railways – who had to sell up entirely.

By the 1880s, when the landed estate as the focus of English country life seemed to be at its zenith, the political and economic power of the landed interest was already in decline. England had changed in the 50 years after the death of George III from a country where the rural population was in the majority to an overwhelmingly urban nation. By the 1880s the great masses of people lived and worked in towns. At the same time a series of parliamentary reform bills to extend the franchise and modernising constituencies, beginning with the great Reform Bill in 1832, had transferred the balance of power in the House of Commons from rural constituencies to the towns. The extension of local government, with the creation of county councils in the 1880s, transferred administration from the landowner to elected public bodies and bureaucrats. New classes of rich and educated urban and industrial men meant the country was no longer dominated by the landed rich as it had been in the eighteenth and early nineteenth centuries.

While modifying the political power represented by the landed estate the impact of all this has been exaggerated. The old landed families continued to play their part in local and national government: the new county councils were run by landowners and the landed classes continued

to play a substantial role in both Houses of Parliament well into the twentieth century. Contrary to expectation, swathes of the newly enfranchised urban working class were Tory and happy to be represented in the Commons by the son of an earl or baronet. Winston Churchill was the grandson of a duke, Harold Macmillan the son-in-law of a duke, Anthony Eden the son of a baronet while David Cameron is the grandson of a baronet and married to the daughter of a baronet. Many of the late-nineteenth century new rich with their industrial or colonial fortunes acquired titles, country houses and large estates. Families such as the Guinnesses (ale), Willses (tobacco), Pearsons (oil), Cayzers (shipping), Vesteys (meat) and Wernhers (gold) were effortlessly integrated into the old landed classes. The Pearsons, Viscounts Cowdray, have been the largest landowners in Sussex for 100 years and the Guinnesses, Earls of Iveagh, the largest in Suffolk for the same period. In the Edwardian age, the landed classes continued to be augmented by very substantial new landowners.

The problem was a more general angst about the purpose and security of a landed estate, which made those who were often still rich and playing a traditional role

⚓ *Many country houses and estates were bought by specialist demolition companies who sold the timber, architectural components, fittings and materials. Costessey Hall, Norfolk, with dismantled wood carvings being prepared for sale after the First World War.*

in national life nevertheless lose their nerve and retreat. The Duke of Sutherland, who sold the Trentham estate in Staffordshire in 1919, was a multi-millionaire while his wife was Mistress of the Robes to Queen Mary. The Earl of Dudley, who sold Witley Court in Worcestershire in 1920, was equally rich and had been Viceroy of Ireland and Governor General of Australia. And so it was not as if he or the duke were suddenly impoverished or ousted from their traditional role in public life – they just thought there was no future in their vast Victorian houses and expensively maintained paternalistic estates. Of course they were wrong, as attested by the fact that in both cases the partially restored Victorian gardens of their erstwhile seats are hugely popular and profitable tourist attractions (and would have been even more so with a house, art collection and resident duke or earl, as Chatsworth so gloriously demonstrates).

From the 1880s onward estates were sold in increasing numbers. In the 1880s and 90s, several leading landowners sold outlying properties often brought in by later marriages or purchase (though usually keeping their principal ancestral estate). The Earl of Ancaster sold his Welsh estates; the Duke of Richmond sold all the Gordon estates in Scotland; the Marquess of Ailesbury sold his Yorkshire estates around Masham; the Marquess of Salisbury sold land in Lancashire and Essex inherited from the Gascoynes and the Duke of Marlborough his Buckinghamshire estate. In some cases these were bought by new money and kept together as estates, otherwise they were broken up and some were sold to the tenant farmers and for building development in areas near towns.

The reasons for the at first sight inexplicable defeatist gloom among the Edwardian upper classes can be found in the policies of the Liberal Party (an institution whose demise turned out to be closer at hand than that of the landed aristocracy): the Liberals had a bee in their bonnet about 'land reform'. In the 1860s there had begun a debate about aristocratic monopoly of landholding. Radical MPs such as John Bright from Manchester believed in this 'monopoly' and began agitating about the subject. It was claimed by the radicals that fewer than 150 men owned half of England. In the belief that such monopoly allegations could not be substantiated, the Earl of Derby (the Tory Prime Minister) supported the idea of a comprehensive survey of landownership and introduced the proposal to the House of Lords in 1872. It was implemented in 1873 as the *Return of Owners of Land*. The *Return* contained many errors and inaccuracies but was the first survey of English landowning since William the Conqueror's Domesday Book of 1086. Some landowners did not know their exact acreages and sent in 'guesstimates', especially in the mountainous areas of northern Britain where estates had never been properly mapped or measured. The large acreages of several Highlands estates turn out to have been exaggerated. Nevertheless, the *Return* gave a useful overall picture of the high-water mark of British private landowning before the impact of social and economic change in the twentieth century.

In fact, the *Return* was used by both traditionalists and radicals to support their arguments: it emerged that more than 900,000 individuals in Britain owned land ranging from a fraction of an acre to a great estate. Numerically, the largest group were 'cottagers' – those who owned large gardens, smallholdings or allotments. They amounted to over 800,000 people. About 43,000 people owned estates of more than 100 acres, including the yeomen and lesser gentry who together owned 40 per cent of all the land in England. About 1,500 greater landowners owned 43 per cent of England (12.5 million acres), including 710 magnates who owned a quarter of the land in England (7 million acres). Institutional landowners owned only 5 per cent of the land in 1873. The distribution of property varied throughout England, but estates were largest in the North and smallest in the Home Counties.

The 1873 *Return*, sometimes dubbed 'the New Domesday', formed the basis for J. Bateman's *The Great Landowners of Great Britain* (the fourth and most complete edition of which was published in 1883). Bateman abstracted and corrected all the landowners recorded as owning more than 3,000 acres in 1873, whether located in a single place or scattered through several counties. The 1883 edition of Bateman provided the most accurate (though not totally accurate) listing of landholding in the late nineteenth century and is the basis of all the estate statistics in works such as the *Complete Peerage* and twentieth-century histories of landowners and landholding. Bateman provides a camera image of the English estate at its zenith, the peak before decline. Where the acreages are given in the present book as in 1883, this information is derived from Bateman. In 1883 there were a total of 1,363 large landowners in England, comprising 331 great landowners (owning over 10,000 acres) and 1,032 greater gentry (over 3,000 acres). To some extent most of Bateman's greatest landowners survive in the twenty-first century but there has been more change and decay in the gentry category. In nearly all cases, however, the size of estates has shrunk, often by as much as 50 per cent, since 1883.

The increasing economic uncertainty facing landowners after the 1880s was therefore exacerbated by radical and Liberal attacks in Parliament on the landed interest and the threat of land taxes or worse, even the possible nationalisation of land. Perhaps even more than the agricultural depression, this frightened people into divesting themselves of land. Between about 1885 and 1920, the radical campaign against 'landed monopoly' had a significant impact on the policies of the great landowners. In 1894, Lord Harcourt, the Liberal Chancellor of the Exchequer, introduced estate duty, with the maximum rate then being 8 per cent on estates worth £1 million, though this was soon to rise. The introduction of death duties by the Liberals is in retrospect the event generally regarded as the most serious threat to landed estates, as it meant that property had to be sold every generation in order to pay the resulting tax. After one or two generations, not enough was left to be economically viable and eventually whole estates were liquidated as a result. Though the rates were not originally onerous, they increased dramatically during both World Wars. The death of heirs in the First World War, as well as sometimes incurring multiple death duties, also discouraged landowners and made them feel it was no longer worth carrying on.

Lloyd George saw landed estates not so much as an important element in the rural economy, to be encouraged at a time of agricultural depression, but as a source of government revenue to be taxed accordingly. In 1909 he sought, unsuccessfully as it turned out, to introduce the 'People's Budget', which included a state valuation of land and a 20 per cent tax on the future 'unearned increment' as well as ¹/₂d in the £1 on the capital value of undeveloped land and minerals. In comparison with the eye-watering rates of taxation in England between 1940 and 1980, these were moderate levies but they were then seen as confiscatory and like all taxes, threatened to become harsher with time. In 1906, the Liberal Government gave county councils compulsory powers to purchase land for smallholdings. This legislation and the resultant political posturing surrounding it was seen as a direct attack on landed society and the landed estate.

The Duke of Bedford's 1909 sale of the Thorney Abbey estate in Cambridgeshire to the individual tenant farmers at very low prices was for political rather than financial reasons. It was in order to disarm criticism of an aristocratic monopoly of landowning and represented a remarkable volte-face. Only 50 years earlier, his Victorian predecessors had spent £566,558 on 'new works and permanent improvements' to the Thorney estate. The dispersal of all the Duke of Sutherland's rich Midlands estates during and after the First World War was also partly political funk after a century of lavish investment and progressive management.

Though the political denunciation of landed estates was confined to the Liberal Party, anti-landed policies crossed political boundaries. The Wyndham Act, breaking up Irish estates in 1903, was passed by A.J. Balfour's Conservative government: a special case, it was intended to assuage demands for Home Rule and independence by offering Irish peasantry the land they tilled. The Wyndham Act compulsorily acquired all tenanted land in Ireland, at fair – even generous – prices, and 'lent' occupiers the money to buy their holdings at negligible rates of interest. In some ways it was part of a Europe-wide reaction against modern industrial and urban society manifested in the revival of folk music, William Morris fabrics, handicrafts, garden cities, subsidised merry peasants and 'the Cotswolds'.

However, in retrospect it is difficult to take any more seriously than Morris dancing and was soon overtaken by the realities of modern economics. (In Northern Ireland estates have been part reconstituted since the 1920s using industrial money, while in the South a new Irish class of lawyers, property developers and 'money men' have also reconstituted some bigger land holdings over the past 30 years. There are few small plots supporting one man and a pig in Ireland today.)

At the time, however, the Wyndham Act caused a frisson of horror and seemed a precedent for possible land nationalisation and expropriation in England, a fear reinforced by the Liberals' powers of compulsory purchase for 'smallholdings'. The fiscal policies of the Liberals, with their threat of worse to come and the dark shadow of land nationalisation advocated by the more ardent reformers and radical theorists as a solution to the 'land question', encouraged landowners to sell at least part of their estates and invest in safer options such as Russian industry (then the world's fastest-growing economy), the colonies, United States equities or South American railways, all of which provided greater financial returns unaffected by the vagaries of English politics. The scares of the Wyndham Act and Lloyd George's programme culminating in the 1909 budget were the background to the accelerated land sales from 1910–14. But it was not all funk, for at the time some of it seemed to be wise management: liquidating landed assets and increasing income by reinvesting capital safely elsewhere.

In the period up until the outbreak of the First World War it has been estimated by F.L. Thompson in *English Landed Society* that 800,000 acres of land were sold (roughly 200 estates): sales, perhaps surprisingly, continued throughout the War. Estates sold in whole or part during the First World War included the Biddlestone estate in Northumberland, parts of Trentham and Lilleshall, the 6,000-acre Amesbury estate of the Antrobus family in Wiltshire (which included Stonehenge) in 1915, the Earl of Derby's 4,000-acre Burscough estate in Lancashire (1916) and Earl Cowper's Wrest Park in Bedfordshire (1917).

THE INTER-WAR YEARS

The War had temporarily increased agricultural production to feed a beleaguered island and the 1917 Corn Production Act guaranteeing prices saw an increase in profitability of farming and land. That was short-lived, however: the Act was repealed in 1921, heralding a further agricultural depression which lasted until 1939 when the outbreak of the Second World War saved English farming through help and subsidies, though of course it was to have a damaging impact in other ways.

Following the peace in 1918, and on the back of the brief wartime revival of agriculture and related increases in land values, there was a flood of estates onto the market. Heather Climenson in her *English Country Houses and Landed Estates* (1982) described the sales of that period as a 'veritable avalanche'. It has been computed, for instance, that a third of the estates in Derbyshire were broken up and lost then, including Glossop, Wingerworth, Sutton Scarsdale, Barlborough and Markeaton. Sales between 1918 and 1920 included the Earl of Harewood's 2,000-acre Stainsby estate in Yorkshire, 8,000 acres comprising the whole of the southern part of the Earl of Pembroke's Wilton estate, Wiltshire, as well as the principal part of the Trentham estate and the Earl of Dudley's Great Witley in Worcestershire. Such an intense lemming rush was possibly in anticipation of the budget of 1919, which raised death duties to 40 per cent on estates over £200,000 in value. By 1939 it rose to 60 per cent and in the 1940s to 90 per cent, but by then new trusts, estate companies and life-time giving had helped to make the tax optional, at least for the prudent and well-advised, or the lucky. It was a perfect demonstration of the effect of the Laffer Curve — the higher the rate of tax, the less collected.

According to the *Estates Gazette* of 31 December 1921, a quarter of the land in England and Wales changed ownership in the three previous years. This was the same proportion as in the sixteenth century when the Church and Crown estates were sold off. Even where the whole of an estate was not sold, individual farmholdings, secondary estates and peripheral outlying land were disposed of, so whetting the appetite. Often 'peripheral sales' presaged the dissolution of a whole estate within a generation, as at the Duke of Sutherland's Trentham and Lilleshall properties in the Midlands that began as peripheral sales, or at Panshanger in Hertfordshire, though the final dissolution of the latter was ultimately due to a lack of any direct male heirs after the death of Lady Desborough in 1952.

The 1920s saw the real break-up and dispersal of the English landed estate. Higher taxation, death duties, the relentless decline in income from landed property, the seeming impermanence of twentieth-century life and cultural pessimism all combined to encourage selling. In elegiac tones, *The Times* wrote in 1920: 'England is changing hands. The sons perhaps lying in far-away graves; the daughters, secretly mourning someone dearer than the brother, have taken up some definitive work away from home and the old people knowing there is no son or near relative left to keep up the old traditions, or so crippled by necessary taxation take the irrevocable step ...'

The Duke of Beaufort sold all his oldest estates — about 25,000 acres — around the ruins of Raglan Castle in Monmouthshire, the original seat of the Herbert family. The Duke of Norfolk sold his Surrey estate near Dorking, which had originated in an inheritance from the Warennes in the early fourteenth century, augmented by the 11th Duke's purchases *circa* 1811. The Earl of Ancaster sold the whole of the beautiful Normanton estate in Rutland, inherited from his Heathcote ancestors, and the house was subsequently demolished. In 1921–24 came the final collapse of Stowe (beginning with the bankruptcy sale of contents in 1848) when the remaining farms and many of the garden ornaments were sold, though the house itself was saved by conversion to a school. This happened in several other cases between the Wars, including Canford, Bryanston and Milton Abbey in Dorset, Wycombe Abbey in Buckinghamshire, the Oratory School at Woodcote in Berkshire and Millfield in Somerset; numerous prep schools also took over unoccupied houses.

In earlier times, when families got into financial difficulties or failed to produce an heir and disposed of their estate, it was often bought *en bloc* by a new owner, as when the Rothschilds bought the Mentmore estate from the Dashwoods in the 1840s, or Waddesdon from the Duke of Marlborough in the 1870s, and the Barings purchased the Stratton Park estate in Hampshire from the Duke of Bedford in the late eighteenth century. Estates had been sold as entities to merchants, lawyers, nabobs, bankers, admirals with Prize Money and — increasingly in the nineteenth century — to rich industrialists, brewers and South African millionaires. This was far less the case after the First World War when agricultural land was no longer seen as a good investment, let alone the best investment, and a landed estate had lost the political clout and patronage it had once conferred. Many new rich people preferred merely to rent a house in the country, a shoot or fishing, or to acquire a sporting estate in Scotland, a yacht and a house in the South of France rather than buy a traditional English estate with all the associated expense and public responsibilities involved. As a result, estates were increasingly broken up rather than sold as a going concern.

An ominous development after the First World War was the emergence of companies who specialised in asset-stripping and the break-up of estates. They would buy a complete property and then make a profit by selling off the

lodges, cottages and farms individually, felling the timber without replanting, demolishing the house and selling the fittings and the lead and timber, even the slates from the roof, leaving uneconomic buildings like Georgian follies and model farms to fall down and building ugly modern 'semi-detached' houses and bungalows on odd plots and road frontages as strips of ribbon development before the Town and Country Planning Act introduced long overdue building controls in 1947. Between 1930 and 1940 the whole county of Middlesex and all its estates (apart from some parks) disappeared under brick and concrete in a decade which, contrary to popular belief, saw the most dynamic and fastest period of growth in the English economy of the twentieth century – although, prior to planning controls, it was exceptionally destructive of the landscape.

From the 1920s to the 1950s, an estate was more valuable dead than alive, in bits rather than as a whole. The breakers posed a great threat to any estate coming onto the market, especially one close to expanding centres of population. Such properties could be bought by property development companies and syndicates, lotted up and sold for house building, hospitals or golf courses. Sometimes the house itself survived as a hotel, a hydro, a nursing home, a school or an old people's institution but the estate landscape with all its beauties was forever destroyed. This happened frequently between the Wars, especially around London, Birmingham or in South Lancashire.

Estates in more remote locations were also threatened. The further away they were, the less likely it was that anybody who had not inherited and loved them would want to live there and keep them going. However, they were attractive to government agencies with powers of compulsory purchase in the 'national interest': the Ministry of Defence in Dorset, Wiltshire and Northumberland, water authorities wanting new reservoirs in the Midlands or the Forestry Commission, set up at the end of the First World War with powers of compulsory purchase and a public mission to cover the hills of Scotland, Wales and northern England with dark evergreen softwood plantations in utilitarian square blocks, ignoring the contours. An estate belonging to a single owner was easier to expropriate than lots of individual smallholdings. Several estates were liquidated in this way, such as the Duke of Northumberland's Kielder estate in the 1930s, where grouse-inhabited, heather-clad moors disappeared to make way for the Forestry Commission's 'largest forest in Europe' and the Kielder Reservoir; or Viscount Fitzalan's Derwent estate in the Derbyshire Peak, which became the Ladybower Reservoir.

⚓⚓ *Tank training in the Second World War on the Downs of the Duke of Norfolk's Arundel Estate in Sussex. The area was requisitioned in 1940.*

WAR AND DESTRUCTION

The Second World War caused immense disruption and destruction on estates. That cataclysmic event seemed to fulfil many of the fears that had threatened estate owners during the previous 50 years: compulsory acquisition by government departments, arbitrary destruction by both sides and the overthrow of all civilised rights of private property. When it became increasingly clear from the mid-1930s that armed conflict with Hitler's Germany was inevitable, the British government belatedly began to re-arm and plan for mobilisation of the nation when war broke out. One aspect was a secret survey of property that could be used in the war effort and a Directorate of Lands and Accommodation was duly set up for the purpose at the Office of Works in Whitehall. A confidential register was compiled on a regional basis to meet the expected wartime requirements of the War Office, Admiralty, Air Ministry, Ministry of Transport, Board of Trade, Food (Defence Plans) Department, Air Raid (Precautions) Department

and other official bodies. In January 1939 the War Office was given precedence for its training units above all other types of requisitioning. The owners were not told that their property had been earmarked for requisitioning and were only given a week's notice when plans were put into operation following the outbreak of war.

As a result, in the early years of the War landowners were often alarmed by the unannounced arrival of a party of officials to survey their property for some mysterious purpose. Gunby Hall and its estate in Lincolnshire was given to the National Trust during the War when the owner, General Massingberd, discovered workmen secretly marking trees in the park to be chopped down for a runway – apparently the whole estate was to be requisitioned and flattened to make way for an airfield. Occasionally, wartime uses were decided by family acquaintance as well as Civil Service diktat. For example, the Duke of Bedford made the Woburn Abbey estate available for the 'hush-hush' activities of the Imperial Intelligence Committee (the predecessor of the Government Communications Headquarters GCHQ) because his cousin, Odo Russell, worked there and asked the Duke if his department could move to Woburn when war broke out. The Duke agreed,

but for most people when notice was served on them in 1939 and 1940, it came as a shock and they were left with little time to prepare and no power to refuse.

Owners were paid compensation equal to the basic rent and minimal damages but this was not enough for full reinstatement after the War. GCHQ, for instance, paid £150 p.a. for the Bletchley Park estate in Buckinghamshire (where the Enigma code was deciphered). However, the amount of land taken varied from property to property: sometimes it was just the main house or outbuildings, in others the park, woodland, cottages, lodges and other areas. At Lowther, the land was requisitioned for tank training and the servants' quarters for billeting soldiers but the main part of the castle was not requisitioned at all, the staterooms drowsing under dustsheets and all the clocks wound weekly by an ancient retainer.

Though country houses, their outbuildings and estates were occupied by schools, hospitals, evacuees, government departments and even used to store evacuated museum treasures, the lion's share was requisitioned by the armed forces for a wide variety of uses from billets and supply bases to strategic signals and training headquarters. Many estates were occupied by successive waves of diverse military organisations of different nationalities, Commonwealth and American troops as well as British. Such men were often rough and vented any ill feelings or high spirits on the property they occupied. Evelyn Waugh in his wartime novels gives a good impression, especially in *Brideshead Revisited*: 'Wonderful old place in its way, pity to knock it about too much.' This was based on his own experiences of being billeted in Kingsdown House, Kent in 1940, which he described as 'derelict surrounded by little asbestos huts . . . one bath for sixty men.' The house was later demolished.

Where houses became military HQs or barracks, the surrounding land was covered with asbestos-roofed, Crittall-windowed Nissen huts on concrete foundations or used for destructive training. The Navy took over several houses in Hampshire. Guards Armoured Division took over the Duncombe estate in Yorkshire; Southern Command, Wilton House – though they moved out of the house itself in 1947, they proceeded to surround that beautiful ancient town with hideous developments on land acquired from the estate and are still entrenched there in 2011. Estates near the south coast, such as Arundel, became part of the coastal defences with huge guns in camouflaged

✢✢ Si Monumentum Requiris. *Manny Shinwell's malicious destruction of Repton's landscape at Wentworth Woodhouse, Yorkshire, by open-cast coal mining for a small quantity of second-rate fuel in 1946.*

redoubts round the cricket ground, tank training on the Downs and one bathroom in the castle reserved for the exclusive use, once a week, of WAAFs from Ford Air Field. At Holkham much of the coastal part of the estate was used for the same purpose, damaging the sea wall with live rounds. The numbers and names of tanks can still be read in faded paint on a brick wall near the house at Holkham: Anson, Atlas, Albatross, Albacore, Albemarle. Dog kennels at Wakehurst Place in Sussex were converted into an underground signals station. Anywhere flat became an airfield, especially in East Anglia, Bedfordshire or west of London. Bomber Command was stationed between London and High Wycombe, where several former estates in Middlesex, like Bentley Priory, still belong to the RAF years after the War ended.

Prior to crossing to Normandy, the British and American Expeditionary Forces were assembled in Kent, Sussex, Hampshire, Wiltshire, Dorset and Somerset.

Troops were billeted in temporary camps and a variety of estate buildings, including stables and cottages. Country houses were turned into officers' messes or battalion headquarters. Amesbury Abbey was used for billeting troops, Longford Castle for trench and camouflage training. Huge military camps were established at Stourhead and Dinton in Wiltshire. Similar encampments were erected on estates in other parts of the country near to strategic railway lines, as at Shugborough in Staffordshire, where one of the remaining wartime huts is still used by the Boy Scouts.

The war damage caused to property by 'friendly' troops is part of English folklore. Many of these stories are true and wartime requisitioning was often the *coup de grâce* to finish off already beleaguered country houses and their estates. The Gopsal estate in Leicestershire, Rufford Abbey (Nottinghamshire) and Warnford Park (Hampshire) were all given up and the houses demolished as a direct result of such depredations. Appuldurcombe on the Isle of Wight, where the house had been empty for some time, was finally wrecked by military occupation. The estate was dispersed and the house reduced to a gutted shell, now in the guardianship of English Heritage. At Arborfield and

Clewer Park in Berkshire the houses were set on fire by troops and the estates given up after the War; Brayton Hall in Cumberland was also totally destroyed by fire and the estate sold off as individual smallholdings. Felix Hall and Belmont Castle in Essex were both gutted and the estates given up, as was North Cray in Kent. Shillinglee in Sussex was burnt by Canadian troops. The incendiary achievements of the military did not just finish off the main house, though. At Slindon, a charming Regency temple was burnt out by the troops stationed on the estate. Many of these fires were inadvertent and caused by discarded stubs, matches or cigarettes (at a time when everybody smoked non-stop) as much as by malicious damage, although the latter was substantial.

General neglect did the most damage. Unblocked gutters and pipes, for example, caused irreparable outbreaks of dry rot. Half the outbuildings at Woburn, including Henry Holland's Riding School and Real Tennis Court, had to be demolished after the War because they were riddled with rot, as was one wing of the house. Of

course, there was also deliberate vandalism: for example, at Dunorlan Park in Kent, the Canadians beheaded all the statues in the garden and Italian prisoners of war did terrible damage at Rufford Abbey in Nottinghamshire, including the use of the silk hangings in the staterooms to make handbags for girlfriends. It was standard to machine-gun the glasshouses and conservatories too, as at Alton Towers in Staffordshire.

Powers of compulsory purchase were enhanced and extended during the Second World War and granted to all sorts of lesser government bodies, such as the Royal Observatory and local education authorities. Sir Philip Sassoon's Trent Park estate in Hertfordshire was compulsorily purchased for a school and the Royal Observatory, having threatened to take the Hinton Ampner estate in Hampshire from its distressed owner Ralph Dutton, acquired Herstmonceux Castle in Sussex instead. After the coal industry was nationalised, the Coal Board could open-cast mine wherever it wanted, as Manny Shinwell (Minister of Fuel in the Attlee government) maliciously demonstrated by wrecking the Repton landscape at Wentworth Woodhouse for a small quantity of poor-quality fuel in 1946. The Wentworth Woodhouse saga has been recounted in Catherine Bailey's *Black Diamonds*. That was not the end of the story, though, for the Fitzwilliam Estates have restored the park, where deer once more roam, new plantations are growing to maturity and all is managed to the highest traditional standards.

In other cases, when properties were returned to the owners they were often so damaged by wartime occupation as to be irreparable: houses burnt or flooded by ill-disciplined soldiery, wrought-iron gates and stone balustraded bridges smashed by jeeps driving through them, all recorded in compensation claims at the Public Records Office, or more amusingly in descriptions in James Lees-Milne's diaries of his tours for the National Trust during and after the War.

Apart from the damage caused, all this helped to induce a sense of pessimism in landowners about the future, especially at the end of the War when the government showed few signs of returning 'temporarily' requisitioned land and it was difficult to repair damaged and neglected estate property because national priorities were building new houses, rebuilding bombed areas and factories. As a result, rationing of materials continued until 1953. In 1939, income tax was raised to 60 per cent (the highest hitherto), with super tax imposed on larger incomes, and taxation grew progressively heavier thereafter in order to fund the War, rising to 90 per cent by 1947.

The unease caused by such events was the background to the flood of estates given up in the 1940s and 1950s. By 1945, which signalled the end of the war, most country estates had reached the nadir of decay: semi-derelict, battered, ill-maintained for six years, ploughed up by tanks, shot at, dotted with the concrete foundations of asbestos and Crittall Nissen huts and other hideous 'temporary' structures. Indeed, many owners soon gave up the unequal struggle and nearly 1,000 country houses were demolished between 1945 and 1955, sometimes to realise the scrap value of the materials. In some cases the owners retained the land and built or adapted a new house; however, in many cases the estate was sold, often in bits to small farmers, developers and breakers (Fornham St Genevieve in Suffolk is a typical example). As in the 1920s, many country houses were bought by specialist break-up companies who felled the timber and sold off anything of value, although the house itself was not always demolished and sometimes continued in its wartime institutional use after the surrounding estate had been sold off. At Himley Hall in Staffordshire (a seat of the Earls of Dudley), after use as a hospital during the War the house became an office of the National Coal Board but the Dudleys (who had lived there until 1940) sold the whole estate after the War and moved to a small place in the Home Counties. Until 1964, Pell Wall in Shropshire continued as a school but the estate went and without it, Sir John Soane's architectural masterpiece has become an increasing problem, now reduced to a shell. The same is true around Britain, from Northumberland to Hampshire, where places such as Ramridge House were never occupied again after requisition by the armed forces during the War.

Other houses were converted to golf clubs or country clubs or hotels when the estates were sold. After the War, some owners sold their English estates and bought land in Kenya or Rhodesia (or even Ireland), foreseeing a more viable long-term future in such places. In 1947, Lord Delamere (who lived in Happy Valley, Kenya) sold the whole of his historic family estate at Vale Royal in Cheshire, which had belonged to his ancestors since the sixteenth century. The estate became the headquarters of the Salt Division of ICI, based at nearby Northwich. Several other Cheshire landowners followed suit, including the Delves-Broughtons at Doddington, who sold all their land except the park and let the house as a girls' school. The Earl of Harrington sold his Derbyshire estate and retreated to the Republic of Ireland, which provided low taxes and good hunting. In 1951, the 4,500-acre Copt Hall estate in Essex was sold to a syndicate. Many places were institutionalised in the 1950s (in Gloucestershire, for instance, 22 such houses). A similar pattern occurred elsewhere but sometimes the estate was retained by the family.

Some estates became prisons, such as Hewell Grange in Worcestershire when the Earl of Plymouth moved to the more manageable Oakley Park estate of his Clive ancestors near Ludlow, sold the farms at Hewell, and the house and park to the Home Office. It remains a prison today, with the prisoners clipping the garden hedges. Stocken Hall in Rutland, which had belonged to the Fleetwood Heskeths in the 1930s, was requisitioned by the RAF in the War, then taken over by the Home Office which ran it as a 'prison-farm', originally bussing in the prisoners from round about to work there. The stable block was converted to pig sties, while ugly new buildings and high wire mesh fences defaced the park. Elsewhere on the former estate, a large new high-security prison has since been constructed. The fine Georgian house, of course, has been left empty and allowed to fall into dereliction, so the public-funded destruction of a once-beautiful estate is comprehensive. Tortworth in Gloucestershire also became a prison, but in this case the Ducie family kept the surrounding estate intact.

SIGNS OF LIFE

After the disasters of the immediate post-war period, the prospects for landed estates began to look rosier from the mid-1950s. By a delicious irony, the Labour Party (though ostensibly more Socialist than the Liberals) saved the English landed estate in the twentieth century from complete destruction after the terrible losses of the first decades. The 'Strange Death of Liberal England' and the rise of the Labour Party as the principal radical element in British politics in the 1920s marked a hiatus in England in playing at peasants and vegetarianism. Labour represented an urban clientele: they were interested in real economics and their aims were the nationalisation of the 'means of production'.

Eager to improve the lives of the urban masses, the Labour Party wanted to nationalise coal, steel and iron; also ship building. They were not interested in side-lines such as nationalising land and so all the seemingly unstoppable anti-estates rhetoric suddenly disappeared from the English political agenda, although Oswald Mosley's British Fascist Party was keen on selling land and anti-estates in some of its rhetoric. The Attlee government after the Second World War introduced a fiscal policy to assist agriculture. In 1945, rebates on income tax were introduced for money spent on agricultural improvements. This encouraged landowners with high taxable incomes to invest in their estates on a scale not seen since before the agricultural depression of the 1870s. These and other positive subsidies and inducements to landowners encouraged the post-war revival in English farming and large increases in the value of land. Even the nationalisation of the coal industry in 1946 proved beneficial for landowners. It freed them of declining and often embarrassing assets, while the compensation was substantial. Reinvested wisely, it introduced a welcome financial injection to many old landed estates in the North and Midlands.

The tyrannical powers of government departments were somewhat curbed after the Crichel Down decision in 1953, when Mrs Marten's Crichel Estate in Dorset successfully defeated the government in court, winning back land compulsorily requisitioned in 1937 by the Air Ministry. As a consequence of this, the Minister of Agriculture in the Conservative government, Sir James Dugdale, resigned. It was a great victory for the private landowner, as a result of which even today an estate has first refusal on the open market of land once acquired compulsorily by the government. The turning point was 1953: gradually those who had not succumbed to terminal despair and had held on at least to the nucleus of family estates found it easier to continue there and to make a living from farming and opening to the public. By the 1980s, a range of commercial activities augmented straightforward public opening. Recreational activities of all kinds occurred: game fairs, horse trials, concerts, holiday lets, as well as conversion of buildings to new uses with redundant farms and stables becoming houses, workshops and offices, or farm shops selling estate produce. This sort of activity has transformed the practicality of many surviving estates and for the first time since the 1870s, English estates have once more become efficient economic units and significant local employers.

Effective protection of listed buildings from 1968 onwards and the more favourable tax system introduced in the 1980s also helped the situation. Competent, well-advised families such as the Devonshires at Chatsworth, Leicesters at Holkham, Salisburys at Hatfield, Norfolks at Arundel, Richmonds at Goodwood, Pembrokes at Wilton, Buccleuchs at Boughton, Northumberlands at Alnwick, or the Tempests at Broughton have set a pace followed by many other estates of various sizes.

It was during this period that many estates were transferred in whole or part to the National Trust, but often with a continuing family connection and always with the promise of good, conservationist management so the transfers can be seen as estate survivals rather than losses. Several historic estates have passed to other kinds of trusts. For example, the West Dean estate in Sussex – comprising 6,000 acres and the whole village – was vested in the Edward James Foundation in 1964. The last Lord Stanhope made the 3,000-acre Chevening estate in Kent into a trust by an Act of Parliament in 1959. Many more estates survive in continuing private ownership although sometimes a combination of trust and private is the case. The last Earl Fitzwilliam left the whole village and park at Wentworth Woodhouse in Yorkshire to a preservation trust and they continue to be managed in conjunction with the agricultural and urban portions of the estate. The ancient royal landholdings – the Crown Estate, the Duchy of Lancaster or the Duchy of Cornwall – also fall more into the category of private estates as they are independently managed, though the proceeds of the Crown Estate go direct to the Treasury with only a percentage to the sovereign.

Nevertheless, the twentieth century saw a continual and steady decline in the overall number and the size of privately owned historic estates. The greatest decline was

✥ *The Donington Park estate in Leicestershire today. East Midlands Airport and Donington Park race track.*

of Bateman's middle-ranking estates: those around the 3,000-acres mark, the landholdings of the gentry rather than of rich landed magnates. These were the most dependent on agriculture and were most affected by the agricultural depression and subsequent Liberal attacks on landholding. Without other large assets, they were most likely to have to sell chunks of their land to pay death duties and other high twentieth-century taxes. While the proportion of land held in estates by great landowners has stayed remarkably stable at about 20 per cent from the fourteenth century to the present day, the proportion owned by lesser landowners or gentry increased from about 25 per cent in the fourteenth century to around 40 per cent in the mid-nineteenth century, but this has subsequently decreased. It is the latter, smaller gentry estates which were mainly lost in the twentieth century, though there were some notable exceptions, such as the total dissolution of the Duke of Sutherland's English estates[2] or the extinction of the Cowper title and lands.

Estates will continue to come and go, like all human institutions, but there are ways to be avoided: the dissolution of Lord Hesketh's rich 11,000-acre Easton Neston estate in Northamptonshire, sold and broken up in 2005, or Luton Hoo in Bedfordshire, sold in 1997 and now a luxury hotel and inevitable golf course.

The most spectacular example in the last half-century of historic landholdings changing hands has not been a private owner but the Church Commissioners. Regency

Tyburnia in London and whole tracts of Kent landscape have been re-developed in a strategy that appeared to prioritise a more 'diverse investment portfolio' over history and tradition. The financial result of such policies has been 'disappointing'. Historic estates which had been conservatively managed by the Church Commissioners for centuries as good solid investments were suddenly liquidated and the proceeds spent on commercial speculation in America, such as warehouse distribution centres in Dallas, and shopping centres in Gateshead and similar places in England.

The Commissioners began selling 'secondary land-holdings' in the 1970s and this whetted their appetite for disposal and change. In 1984, they still owned 172,819 acres in England but nearly half of that disappeared within a decade. In the 1980s, 208 farms were sold (many of which had belonged to the Church since the Middle Ages). Most of the money raised was used to plug holes caused by commercial investments. Prime London property with long-term potential included the freehold of Paddington Station, sold to British Rail for £43,000. In 2009, the Commissioners lost £40 million on a single residential development in New York, according to the *Daily Telegraph*. But the commercial activities of the Church Commissioners and the management of their estates are not subject to the scrutiny of the parliamentary Audit Commission and are also exempt from the Freedom of Information Act.

The present work, however, is focussed not on the historic institutional estates of bodies such as the Church, the Crown, Oxford Colleges, City Livery Companies and ancient charities, but on private landowners and the fate of private landed estates.

Felling the Ancient Oaks illustrates the stories of 21 estates that for various reasons came to an end in the twentieth century and whose fates are characteristic of the tale as a whole. Many others could equally have been chosen, but these particular properties are especially well recorded in the photographic archives of *Country Life*, old sales catalogues and the files of the National Monuments Record. They include properties liquidated because of the extinction of their owner-families or the death of heirs, such as Biddlestone in Northumberland, Panshanger in Hertfordshire and Hinton St George in Somerset; the victims of individual extravagance and incompetence such as Lathom in Lancashire or Donington in Leicestershire; rearrangement of family assets and retreat from land in the face of the perceived Liberal threat to the aristocracy as at Trentham; the encroachment of industry or coal

2   The old Duke of Sutherland's estates; the present Duke (descended from the Earls of Ellesmere) still owns the Ellesmere estates in different parts of England as well as Mertoun in the Scottish Borders.

mining as at Glossop, Beaudesert and Nuttall, or suburban development as at the Deepdene or Cassiobury; also the destructive impact of wartime requisitioning by the military, as at Fornham in Suffolk or Shillinglee in Sussex, or natural disasters like fire at Great Witley and Highhead. In many cases the end was precipitated by a combination of several of these factors converging at once.

Despite the losses, a large number of landed estates in England have survived and many quietly thrived over the last 30 years or more. Depending on definitions, as much as half of rural England is still composed of traditional estates. As F.M.L. Thompson, the leading historian of modern English landowning, stated in an address to the Royal Historical Society 20 years ago: 'In 1989 the thousand-year-old land pattern was still in existence, somewhat dented and battered to be sure but little more battered than it had been fifteen years earlier. It would certainly be unwise to equate the destruction of a pre-1914 country house with the disappearance of the family, which had lived in it or the landed estate, which supported it. What has happened since the First World War is something far short of the collapse or catastrophe which has been over-dramatised

✝ *This motorway service station on the M6 in Staffordshire adorns the Hilton Park estate where the eighteenth-century house, amazingly, still survives converted to offices.*

by many commentators.' But the fact that up to a third of established landed estates in England have disappeared in the past 100 years is still a matter for deep regret: areas which have lost their historic estates, such as west Cumberland or swathes of Wales, have suffered damage to their landscape and their economic prosperity. The current danger in the twenty-first century is that too commercial and speculative an approach to management – rather than neglect and ruin or political interference and high taxes, as was the case in the last century – risks wrecking the landed estate. Much has been lost – as the illustrations in this book demonstrate – which could have played a significant economic and cultural role in contemporary life, while helping to balance and mitigate the peculiarly hideous and irredeemable quality of provincial urban existence in modern England.

By instructions from The Marquess of Anglesey.

STAFFORDSHIRE

In the Parishes of Longdon, Cannock Wood, Hednesford, Norton Canes, Burntwood, and Rugeley.

About 4 miles from Lichfield, and 4 from Rugeley, and within easy distance of the County Town of Stafford and the populous centres of Birmingham and Wolverhampton.

THE EXTENSIVE RESIDENTIAL AND SPORTING

BEAU DESERT ESTATE

comprising:

THE IMPORTANT COUNTY SEAT

"BEAU DESERT HALL"

An Imposing Tudor Mansion,

containing a wealth of old oak panelling, standing about 600 feet above sea level, in a grandly undulating and well-timbered Park.

BEAUTIFUL GARDENS

with Charming Old-world Lawns, Ornamental Yew Hedges, Rock Gardens, Lily Ponds, Trout Pools and Plantations.

A CHARMING COUNTRY RESIDENCE, "Chestall House and Farm"

SEVERAL CAPITAL DAIRY FARMS

NUMEROUS LODGES and COTTAGES　　　TWO EXCELLENT BUNGALOWS

GARDENS with extensive Glass Houses

THE WELL-KNOWN BEAU DESERT GOLF LINKS

THE CASTLE RING (an Ancient Rampart)

ACCOMMODATION LANDS and VALUABLE BUILDING SITES

EXTENSIVE WOODLANDS

many of the Lots with vacant possession; the whole Estate extending to about

2,010 ACRES

To be sold by auction (unless sold in the meantime by private treaty) by

Messrs. W. S. BAGSHAW & SONS

(in conjunction with Messrs. LOFTS & WARNER)

At the SWAN HOTEL, LICHFIELD

on

THURSDAY, THE 13th DAY OF OCTOBER, 1932

at 2.0 p.m.

Beaudesert

STAFFORDSHIRE

The Seat of the Pagets, Earls of Uxbridge and Marquesses of Anglesey, from 1546 to 1935

Situated high up on Cannock Chase near to Rugeley, Beaudesert was surrounded by the Cannock and Rugeley Colliery Company's slag heaps and coal mines (the source of the family wealth) and other modern monstrosities. Even so, it is surprising that an estate with such a long continuous history, a large and romantic Tudor country house in excellent condition and a wild, wooded medieval park should have been abandoned in the 1930s. But the 6th Marquess of Anglesey who owned it had two major properties: Beaudesert, the original Paget seat in Staffordshire, and Plas Newydd, inherited from the Bayleys (his male-line ancestors) on the Isle of Anglesey in Wales. The latter was in a spectacularly beautiful position overlooking the Menai Straits and the mountains of Snowdonia. With its well-proportioned light and spacious rooms, the Wyatt house there seemed the preferable option for the family when the 6th Marquess retrenched after the First World War.

Beaudesert and the Staffordshire lands were the classic example of a sixteenth-century estate built up by Tudor 'new men' out of church land. Originally, it had been a manor and hunting park of the Bishop of Lichfield. It incorporated part of the medieval building at the back. In 1546 it was acquired by Sir William Paget: Secretary of State to Henry VIII, he had accompanied the King to the Field of the Cloth of Gold. Nicknamed 'Catchpole' by the old nobility because he was descended from manorial servants, Paget was one of the new sixteenth-century class of able Court officials and administrators who did well under the Tudors and augmented the nobility in due course. He was created Lord Paget of Beaudesert and his Georgian successors through the female line (the Bayleys of Plas Newydd, who took the Paget name and arms) were advanced to Earls of Uxbridge and Marquesses of Anglesey. The house at Beaudesert was built in 1573–83 by the 3rd Lord Paget and was a large E-plan brick pile with huge mullion windows and ogee-capped turrets. It was described in 1593 as 'a very fair brick house'. The most famous member of the family was the 1st Marquess, a cavalry officer under Sir John Moore at Corunna and Wellington at Waterloo (where his leg was shot off by a cannon ball). Wellington: 'Good God, Paget, your leg's blown off!' Paget: 'I'm damned if it isn't!' He was promoted to full General and Field Marshal.

According to Bateman in 1883, the Plas Newydd estate was 10,000 acres and the Staffordshire estates at Beaudesert and Burton-on-Trent 17,500 acres. The latter, with their coal mines and ironworks, had brought in an enormous income of £100,000 a year in the 1880s, but the 6th Marquess's eccentric and dissolute predecessor, the 'Dancing Marquess', had wrecked the family fortune and bankrupted himself with uncontrolled spending on

☝ *The Dancing Marquess of Anglesey wearing one of his less elaborate outfits. He died bankrupt in Monte Carlo, 1904.*

jewels and other extravagances, dramatics and wild frolics. He died in Monte Carlo in 1904, with personal debts of £544,000. At the subsequent bankruptcy sale his jewels and extraordinary clothes were sold for £88,000, but this was only a fraction of the money he had frittered away on them.

Nevertheless, the settled estates survived, and the 6th Marquess was of a very different stamp. He and his family were prominent members of the Souls, the Edwardian aristocratic group with aesthetic, literary and intellectual interests that included the Lindsays, Mannerses, Herberts, Wyndhams, as well as leading political luminaries such as Arthur Balfour and Lord Curzon. Lord Anglesey embarked on the revival of his houses and estates after inheriting. Following a fire at Beaudesert in 1909, he undertook a lavish restoration of the Elizabethan house aimed at returning the Georgianised interior to its original Tudor character with oak panelling, ornamental plaster ceilings, great hall and long gallery. This restoration was completed in 1912, but the First World War and increased taxation changed everything: Lord Anglesey ceased to use Beaudesert in 1920, and in 1924 attempted to sell the house and its surrounding estate but there were no takers. With the house closed up, Beaudesert remained in limbo for the next 10 years, while Plas Newydd took its place in the family affections, being redecorated by the English artist and designer Rex Whistler and maintained in great luxury.

Having failed to sell Beaudesert as a whole or to find any alternative use for the house, the 6th Marquess finally decided to break up the estate – selling it off in separate lots – and to demolish the house. The main part of the Beaudesert estate was put up for sale in October 1932 and auctioned off in several lots by Bagshaw & Sons of Uttoxeter in the Swan Hotel at Lichfield. It encompassed property in the parishes of Longdon, Cannock Wood, Hednesford, Norton Canes, Burntwood and Rugeley (the latter all being centres of coal mining). In the sales particulars, Beaudesert was described as an 'extensive residential and sporting estate comprising the important county seat "Beau Desert Hall".' However, the house itself again failed to sell. The auctioneer expatiated on the 'beautiful gardens', numerous lodges and cottages, 'extensive woodlands', the 'charmingly undulating park' and, with a harsh breath of realism, 'valuable building sites'.

The outbuildings included a Saw Mill and Pump House, and the estate owned its own golf course, laid out in 1911 on heathland by Herbert Fowler. It was let to a local club, who bought it at the sale. The story is that two members bid

each other up to double the price but Lord Anglesey let the club have it for the original valuation of £2,000, which was all they could afford. The huge kitchen gardens, laid out in the eighteenth century and expanded in the nineteenth, were then notable for their 'immense quantity of greenhouses', now all gone. These included six Carnation and Orchid Houses, a vast range of Vine Houses (186 feet long), a range of Peach and Fig Houses (also 180 feet long) and a Palm House measuring 70 x 35 feet. Only the brick outer garden walls still survive. The New Park covered 333 acres and was enlivened with trout pools; the surrounding agricultural estate was 2,000 acres (the forestry land had already been taken by the Forestry Commission). The farms and cottages were mainly brick and half-timbered. Older ones were described as 'picturesque' and The Nook at Longdon as 'a choice cottage holding' (it has since been demolished). The paternalist system about to come to an end was attested by the fact that the rates on many of these dwellings had been paid directly by the estate and not by the tenants themselves.

The future was foreshadowed by the emphasis on speculative building development in Bagshaw's particulars. Lot 9, 'a corner piece of woodland', was described as 'suitable for a building site'. Gentleshaw Cricket Field was nearing the end of its lease and therefore suitable for development. Lot 40 was 'a corner building site', as was Lot 41, 'having a long road frontage', ideal for ribbon development. Lot 43 consisted of two acres of small enclosures 'forming a building site', while Lot 44 – a 'block of land' of 35 acres – was suitable for building sites. Hagley Farm (Lot 60, with 146 acres) was 'conveniently situated adjacent to the town of Rugeley, having extensive road frontages affording excellent building sites, and forming a valuable building estate with great prospects of development in the near future'.

The announcement of the final demolition of the house in July 1935 'caused uproar'. The Friends of Cannock Chase, the local preservation society, held a protest meeting on the front lawn. In response, Lord Anglesey presented 123 acres of the medieval park, with its ancient trees, to the Friends for preservation as an open space but otherwise went ahead with the demolition and the dispersals. A sale of the fixtures and fittings of the house raised £8,000. The house itself was sold to a Leicester demolition firm for a mere £800.

Today all that survives architecturally is the Grand Lodge, a splendid Jacobean design with a central turreted gatehouse, screen walls and flanking towers, designed in 1820 by Joseph Potter of Lichfield, the County Surveyor

⚓ *The house before demolition in 1936. It was built by the 3rd Lord Paget in 1573 incorporating parts of a medieval hunting lodge of the Bishops of Lichfield. The towering brick elevation with large mullion windows made it an important piece of Elizabethan architecture.*

⚓ *The Grand Lodge at the main entrance to the park was designed in 1820 by Joseph Potter of Lichfield for the 1st Marquess of Anglesey. Its architecture charmingly mimicked that of the main house. It alone survives today converted to a private residence after the demolition of the house.*

⚓ *The hamlet at Longdon comprised a green surrounded by picturesque half-timbered cottages let at low rents while the rates were paid by the estate. They were sold off individually and have been altered subsequently or demolished.*

❦ *'The Nook' at Longdon before and during demolition. It was described in the Sales Particulars in 1932 as 'a choice cottage holding'.*

and former amanuensis of James Wyatt, both of whom had remodelled the interior of the house in the reign of George III. The lodge is now converted, not very sensitively, into a private house, while part of the Upper Park and the old walled garden are used as a campsite by the Scouts and other groups. The overgrown area of the 3rd Lord Paget's proud brick Elizabethan mansion is marked by a ruined fragment thought to be a remnant of the Bishop of Lichfield's medieval hall, with a couple of Perpendicular windows, therefore left in a spasm of archaeological piety during the 1936 demolition. Much of the ancient timber on the estate has been felled. The picturesque old half-timbered and brick cottages round the green at Longdon were all sold off individually and some have

been subsequently altered or demolished. The fringes of the estate are covered with bits of mid-twentieth century ribbon development, the road frontages having been sold for that purpose.

Beaudesert and the Pagets' other Staffordshire estate around Burton-on-Trent, originally the lands of the Benedictine Burton Abbey, acquired at the Dissolution by Sir William Paget, have been largely alienated, though Lord Anglesey remains Lord of the Manor of Burton-on-Trent and still owns some property there, including the Burton Club. But the estate office in the old manor house at Burton has been sold, James Wyatt's neo-Classical Market House and town hall of 1769–70, with the Paget arms in Coade Stone, demolished. Sinai Park at Branston, a medieval timber-framed manor house (originally a summer retreat of the Abbot of Burton and occupied after the Reformation by the Pagets' land agents and stewards) has been empty and derelict for over 50 years. In the 1960s part of it was used as pigsties.

The story of Beaudesert and the Burton estate is a striking demonstration of the impossibility of the planning system to plug the gap and hold things together once an old estate was abandoned and fragmented; the buildings demolished or mutilated, and the landscape part built

⚓𝒷𝓏 *Beaudesert after demolition in 1936. A few masonry fragments of the medieval episcopal hunting lodge were left for antiquarian reasons. Part of the Old Park was presented by Lord Anglesey to the Friends of Cannock Chase in 1936 and is now a popular camp site. Much land has been dotted with suburban houses or Forestry Commission conifers.*

over and degraded. Despite all this much of the area of the former estate survives as open heath land, with sweeps of forestry, and the hills rise to 800 feet above sea level, with striking views over the Trent valley, Rugeley power station and the Midlands landscape from vantage points such as the Castle Ring Iron Age hill fort and Rawnsley Hills. The natural grandeur of scale and wildness helps to absorb the twentieth-century architectural losses and blots.

The 123-acre area of the old park and the walled garden, which Lord Anglesey offered for preservation in 1936, were opened in 1938 and now belong to the Beaudesert Trust, a private trust which maintains the area as woods and glades, with camping facilities for 1,500 visitors. It is a popular attraction for families and young people. Together with the golf course and Forestry Commission plantations, it helps to maintain a flavour of the former estate landscape, even if some of the old cottages have since been replaced with hideous modern houses. The coal mines are now closed, the slag heaps grassed over, the air no longer blackened with smoke and Beaudesert would indeed be a delightful 'residential and sporting estate' and 'county seat' if it still existed, and if the 3rd Lord Paget's great brick house still surveyed its old domain.

Biddlestone

NORTHUMBERLAND

The Seat of the Selby Family from 1311 to 1918

A former stronghold in Border warfare, a centre of tenacious recusant Catholicism and latterly, a model Victorian estate, the main witness today of the old Biddlestone estate is an isolated Catholic chapel in the shell of a fourteenth-century pele tower perched in the foothills of the Cheviots, above the ravine of the Biddle Burn from which it takes its name. Surrounding Forestry Commission plantations of dark Sitka spruce have blanketed the Georgian parkland setting. The austere square stone, three-storey late-Georgian house of the Selby family, to the back wing of which the chapel was once attached, was demolished over 50 years ago. The demolition of Biddlestone Hall in 1957 was the final stage in the dissolution of this romantic, remote estate, 800 feet above sea level in the remote Northumberland moorland of Upper Coquetdale. It marked the end of one of the rare instances of an English estate with a continuous male-line descent for 600 years. Biddlestone had belonged to the Selbys since the reign of King Edward II in the early fourteenth century.

Biddlestone's early history was inextricably linked to the turbulent, blood-stained, war-like character of the long fought-over frontier between England and Scotland. The Selbys were typical Borders landowners, originally soldiers and freebooters, 'alternately defending and plundering', switching their allegiance between England and Scotland

The austere square stone, three-storey late-Georgian house of the Selby family, to the back wing of which the chapel was once attached, was demolished over 50 years ago.

In 1908 the house was described as 'having the air of having been transported by magic from some city clubland and being very surprised to find itself standing on a green bank in Coquetdale!'

in the ups and downs of the Anglo-Scottish wars. They are recorded in the area from the thirteenth century and acquired Biddlestone in 1311, when Walter Selby of Seghill received half the lands there as a result of his marriage to Katherine, daughter of Eustace Delaval of Biddlestone. Sir Walter Selby was a war-like character and having been captured at a siege by King David II of Scotland in 1346, he was summarily beheaded. After this hiccup, the younger son John eventually recovered his father's share of the Biddlestone estate and probably built the original fortified pele tower on the site which part survives as the chapel; the other half of the Biddlestone lands was acquired by the Selbys from the Delavals in 1576, thus uniting the whole township in Selby possession. At that time, the pele tower was extended by wings, a courtyard and gateway to make a more peaceful Elizabeth house. In this form it became the model for 'Osbaldistone Hall', a Catholic manor house in Sir Walter Scott's *Rob Roy*, Scott having visited the area as a young man and stayed at the Rose & Thistle in nearby Alwinton. The romantic, remote character of the estate made a strong impression. He described Biddlestone as 'a large and antiquated edifice peeping out from a Druidical grove of huge oaks' with a 'quadrangle, resembling the inside of a convent, or of one of the older and less splendid colleges of Oxford', and the surrounding estate as 'romantic and wild scenery' amid the 'frowning majesty of the Cheviots . . . a desert district possessing a character of its own'.

This hoary edifice was replaced (except for the pele chapel) in 1796 by Thomas Selby, with 'a neat modern residence' forming an unadorned, rectangular three-storey block of ashlar stone, six bays by five. Further work was done in 1820 for Thomas's son, another Walter Selby, to the design of John Dobson of Newcastle, who improved the interior and may have designed the stables and other outbuildings. Solid model cottages, the Home Farm and kennels followed in the nineteenth century. The house, though, was not of any great character and its Regency severity belied the long history of the place. Madeleine Hope Dodds in her *History of Northumberland* in 1908 described the house as having 'nothing romantic about it and with its severe masonry and plate glass windows [it] has the air of having been transported by magic from some city clubland and being very surprised to find itself standing on a green bank in Coquetdale.'

23 Sir Walter Scott described the surrounding estate as 'romantic and wild scenery' amid the 'frowning majesty of the Cheviots . . . a desert district possessing a character of its own'.

The chapel, however, represents a continuous Catholic tradition from the Middle Ages. Like many northern gentry, the Selby family did not conform to the Established Church after the sixteenth-century Reformation but continued to worship secretly in this remote spot, maintaining Benedictine or Jesuit priests at Biddlestone for themselves and the local community. They created the present more prominent mid-Victorian Gothic Revival chapel within the thick walls of their ancient tower following the Catholic Emancipation Act of 1829, which removed all legal restrictions against Catholics practising their religion in England.

The Catholic tradition of the Selbys meant that they had to pay fines and double land taxes and meet other special liabilities in the late sixteenth, seventeenth and early eighteenth centuries, so were never very rich, though successive marriages to coal-owning and West Indian Plantation-owning heiresses in the eighteenth century enabled them to part revive their fortunes and expand their land-holdings. A succession of Victorian squires played their role as landowners, Justices of the Peace and High Sheriffs, and built solid stone farms and cottages for their tenants. The estate, however, as well as being remote, was largely moorland and less valuable than smaller estates in richer farming country and this, as well as the personal inclinations of the final owner, may have mitigated against survival in the twentieth century.

By the time of Bateman's *Great Landowners of Great Britain* in 1883, the Selbys were recorded as owning 30,000 acres worth £10,000 a year in Northumberland, centred on Biddlestone (Earl Cowper had an income six times this amount on estates of similar extent in the South). However, already by 1914 this large acreage and the resulting income had been reduced by nearly half to 17,000 acres worth £5,693 p.a., no doubt partly due to the agricultural depression but also because of land sales. In 1911, Walter Arthur Selby, the last member of the family to own Biddlestone, sold the moors at the western end of the estate, including Carshope, Windy Heugh, Bygate Hill and Wilkwood to the War Office for the new Otterburn Military Training Camp, which still occupies the area. He subsequently tried unsuccessfully to let the house and shooting rights before selling most of the main part of the estate, including the agricultural land in Coquetdale, in 1914 to Frederick Beavan. Finally, the nucleus including the Hall itself and 500 acres was sold by auction in the County Hotel, Newcastle to Farquhar Deuchar of the brewing family on 26 June 1918, just before the end of the First World War.

The First World War was not the best time to sell a

⚜ *The house was used as a convalescent home for soldiers during the Second World War.*

All that was left was the chapel which was used by the small local Catholic community, who saved it from general dissolution.

country house and landed property so the 36-year-old Lieutenant-Commander Selby's decision to sever this historic family link with such a strong recusant tradition cannot have been a strictly financial move. He had inherited the house from his father in 1900, aged 18, but never lived at Biddlestone and the inference is that his decision was a young man's personal inclination, that he did not like the place, and with no son of his own saw no future. Instead he preferred to pursue his naval career and to live comfortably in the South of England, not the wilds of Northumberland.

The Hall and parkland have subsequently changed hands several times. Following the successive sales at the time of the First World War, the estate was broken into smaller units, some being sold to farmers and much to the Forestry Commission, who blanketed the surroundings with dead evergreen plantations. The house was used as a convalescent home for soldiers during the Second World War. Afterwards, it was never occupied again and was demolished in 1957, leaving only the chapel long used by the small local Catholic community, who saved it from general dissolution. Following the departure of the Selbys, the Diocese of Hexham and Newcastle leased the chapel from the Forestry Commission. It remained in regular use, served by the parish priest from Thropton until 1992, when the lease was surrendered. Happily, it now belongs to the Historic Chapels Trust, which has restored this remaining historic building, where the Latin Mass Society still celebrates occasional Masses.

The loss of the house itself – decent but dull architecture – is not the main thing to be lamented at Biddlestone. Rather it is the severing of the ancient traditions and romantic character of the estate, and the long male-line descent. A large quarry eats away at the hill behind. Nothing survives of Walter Scott's druidical oaks, or the romantic Picturesque park planting shown in old photographs and postcards. A beautiful and ancient wooded landscape has been transformed into an area of utilitarian forestry and no visible trace remains of the Regency quadrangular stables, nor the tall stone house, nor the carefully tended grounds of the Selby family. Only the lonely little chapel remains, tucked away up a muddy track through the spruce trees, still remote from the world.

The demolition of Biddlestone Hall in 1957 was the final stage in the dissolution of this romantic, remote estate, 800 feet above sea level in the remote Northumberland moorland of Upper Coquetdale. It marked the end of one of the rare instances of an English estate with a continuous male-line descent for 600 years.

Cassiobury

HERTFORDSHIRE

Seat of the Capels, Earls of Essex, and their Morrison Ancestors from 1546 to 1922

Cassiobury, northwest of Watford in Hertfordshire, is an example of an estate on the edge of a rapidly growing town, which gave in to the inexorable urban pressure and was largely built over with modern housing in the course of the twentieth century. It belonged to the Capels, Earls of Essex, from the early seventeenth to the early twentieth century. Arthur Capel of Hadham inherited the estate through his wife, the daughter and heiress of Sir Charles Morrison. Following the Dissolution of 1546, the Morrisons had been granted the former monastic property. Sir Charles Morrison I had begun the Tudor H-plan house, which was completed by his son Charles Morrison II, who succeeded him in 1556. Arthur, 1st Earl of Essex, Lord Lieutenant of Ireland and an ambitious courtier in the reign of Charles II, substantially reconstructed this Tudor house to the design of his kinsman Hugh May in 1674–75. The interior was notable for rich staterooms, with Grinling Gibbons' carvings, similar to those at Windsor Castle, and Lord Essex carried out the lavish reconstruction of his house in the hope that Charles II might visit him there. This never happened. He also planted the estate with long straight avenues and formal blocks of woodland, putting into practice the advice of his friend John Evelyn in *Sylva* (1664). The reconstructed

⚹ *The main lodge designed by James Wyatt in delightful Gothic in 1802 was demolished by road engineers in 1967 to make way for a 'new traffic system'.*

⚹ *Cassiobury was demolished in 1927 and sold for the value of its building materials. The park is now largely a suburb of Watford covered with 1930s semis.*

⚓ *The house dated from the sixteenth century with magnificent Baroque interiors created by Hugh May in 1674. It was externally gothicked by James Wyatt for the 5th Earl of Essex circa 1800.*

seventeenth-century house and the 1st Earl's plantations are recorded in a bird's-eye engraving by Kip and Knyff in *Britannia Illustrata* or *Les Délices de la Grande Bretagne* (1707).

The whole place was substantially remodelled by the 5th Earl of Essex, Lord Lieutenant of Hertfordshire, *circa* 1800. James Wyatt reconstructed the exterior of the house in the Gothic style, adding cloisters and outbuildings to match, in the hope of restoring Cassiobury to its

abbatial appearance. At the same time, Humphry Repton landscaped the park, making a feature of the Grand Union Canal, which had been constructed through the estate in 1790 and was England's principal transport route between London and the industrial Midlands. Repton liked to have signs of activity in his landscapes and the barges and locks on the canal were ideal. At the same time a quadrangular Home Farm with weather-boarded buildings was constructed to a model plan and Gothic stables and lodges to James Wyatt's design. Other estate buildings were added by Jeffry Wyatville, *circa* 1817, including a trellised orangery, Swiss Cottage (inhabited by the Under-Butler

access to walk in the park, but not to have picnics there. This was a common convention and the parks of Arundel, Hatfield, Blenheim and Alnwick are still open free to local residents today.

By the standards of Victorian aristocrats, the Earls of Essex were not especially rich. According to Bateman, their Hertfordshire estate was 5,545 acres, and their total acreage including land in Essex was 10,000 acres. The 6th Earl of Essex enriched the house with fine collections of books and pictures, but on his death in 1892 financial difficulties became apparent. In 1893 Christies held a sale of some pictures, books, porcelain and furniture from the house and Cassiobury was let furnished for a time.

Like several cash-strapped English peers of the time, the 7th Earl of Essex married a rich American wife, Adèle, the eldest daughter of Beach Grant of New York City, and her money helped to support Cassiobury's early-twentieth century swansong when *Country Life* recorded the place, lavishly maintained and full of flowers, and enthused about its seeming detachment from the busy modern world of the Edwardian age. The *Country Life* author enthused about 'the delightful grounds' and 'grandly timbered park'. 'Therein is peace and quiet; the aloofness of the old-world country home far from the haunts of men reigns there still, and Watford and its rows of villas and its busy streets is forgotten as soon as the lodge gates are passed.'

But Watford, situated on the main line from London to Birmingham, was growing rapidly with new industry and spreading twentieth-century suburbs. In 1908, 184 acres of the Cassiobury estate were sold to a syndicate for building in a sign of things to come. The 7th Earl died, aged 59, in 1916 as a result of being run over by a taxi, provoking a hefty bill for death duties. His widow sold up in 1922. There was a huge sale of the contents of the house lasting 10 days and the core of the estate was put on the market by Humbert & Flint in association with Knight Frank & Rutley in June 1922. The Sales Particulars announced: 'By direction of the Right Honourable Adèle, Countess Dowager of Essex' the 'Cassiobury Park Estate including the Historical Family Mansion, Little Cassiobury, and the West Herts Golf Links, embracing in all an Area of about 870 acres.'

A truncated bit of the park, about 190 acres, was acquired by Watford Council for public recreation and survives as Watford Park, with the golf club to the west. It contains Repton's surviving lake. Most of the land was bought by a development syndicate for building, though. The big house, as so often, failed to find a new occupier and was finally demolished for its materials in 1927: 'To lovers of the antique, architects, builders etc., 300 tons of

in the 1888 census), Russell Cottage and several *cottages ornés* and other characteristic Picturesque dependencies. An ancient water mill and a scenic wooden bridge over the River Gade provided other popular 'beauty spots' on the estate for the generation of Constable and Turner to admire. Late nineteenth-century photographs show the place in full maturity, with ancient oak and elm trees and Repton's plantations enhancing the scene.

In the 6th Earl's time the park played host to many local activities: Victorian cricket matches, the Watford Horticultural Show and parades of the Hertfordshire Yeomanry. The inhabitants of Watford were given free old oak; 100 very fine old beams and 10,000 Tudor period bricks.' The Grinling Gibbons carvings, valued at £20,000, were sold mainly to American museums. Construction of the residential Cassiobury Estate began. The land was made subject to restrictive covenants, stipulating that only good-quality detached or semi-detached houses would be allowed. Most of these were built in the 1930s, although building has gone on continuously ever since, with much recent 'infill' housing on former back gardens. Suburban housing covers most of the estate today. Sales of the outer parts of the estate for building continued throughout the 1920s and into the 1930s. Whippendell Woods were sold to the council in 1935 to add to Watford's open recreation space.

ଌ ⚓ ଌ

ଌ The mediaeval water mill on the River Eade was consciously retained as a picturesque feature of the estate landscape by Repton. This late-nineteenth century photograph creates a Constable-like picture.

⚓ Fishermen with nets on the River Gade which ran through the park, as did the Grand Union Canal constructed in 1790.

Picturesque scenes on the River Gade in the park, including the Chinese Bridge and ancient mill, all now demolished and built over.

⚓ ⚓ *The formal gardens round the house were embellished thanks to the American fortune of the 7th Earl's American wife Adèle, daughter of Beach Grant of New York City. They were noted for specimen trees, roses and decorative sculpture. Such* Country Life *photographs captured Cassiobury's Indian Summer.*

This fate seemed inevitable in the 1920s, once Cassiobury ceased to be an aristocratic country house, for an area situated within one minute of Watford Junction railway station. The *Estates Gazette* in 1922 declared unsentimentally that Cassiobury provided 'the best and most rational area for the expansion of Watford.' It was ripe for development. Many of the estate buildings, as well as the main house, have been demolished, including Wyatville's orangery and *cottages ornés*, the Home Farm and the old Mill. James Wyatt's stable block remains in Richmond Drive, converted to an old people's home and renamed Cassiobury Court. The former dower house at Little Cassiobury was converted to the South West Hertfordshire Education Department's offices. In Pevsner's view, it is the 'best classical house in Watford', dating from the seventeenth century. In the 1930s, it was rehabilitated by Clough Williams Ellis; the adjoining Technical College of 1938 by Lanchester & Lodge is a handsome neo-Georgian design so here at least was some cultural compensation for the losses.

James Wyatt's delightful castellated main entrance lodge of 1802 survived until 1967, when it was demolished by road engineers to make way for a 'new traffic system'. The Grand Union Canal now wends its way past 1930s semis. Street lights have replaced the ancient oaks and elms once recorded in fine aquatints based on watercolours by Turner and Pugin in John Britton's *Cassiobury Park Hertfordshire, The Seat of the Earl of Essex*, published in 1837. It was reprinted in facsimile in 2005 and is the best monument to a beautiful lost estate landscape. The 8th Earl of Essex eventually emigrated to the warmer climes of the Caribbean and was last heard of in the 1960s, living in a house called 'Little Cassiobury' in Jamaica.

❧ *The Orangery of 1817 by Jeffry Wyattville, now demolished.*

⚘ *James Wyatt's castellated stables, now known as Cassiobury Court, survive as an old people's home in a suburban street named Richmond Drive.*

Chicksands

∽ BEDFORDSHIRE ∽

Seat of the Osborn Family, Baronets, from 1576 to 1936

For over 70 years, the Chicksands estate has been a 'hush-hush' defence establishment. On 15 April 1936 the Crown Commissioners bought the estate on behalf of the RAF as part of the pre-war campaign of re-armament in the face of the threat from Hitler's Germany. The house itself was briefly let to Gerald Bagshaw but was requisitioned by the Royal Navy in 1940. After nine months the RAF took over operations there and established a signal intelligence collection unit (known as 'Y station') at RAF Chicksands Priory. The estate played an important role in the Second World War, intercepting German signals. (The material was passed from Chicksands for interpretation at the Government Code and Cypher School at Bletchley Park in Buckinghamshire, famous as the place where the German Enigma code was broken by a team of brilliant boffins.)

After the War in 1950, Chicksands was sub-leased to the United States Air Force. It served as the base of the American 6940th Radio Squadron, a signals intelligence station, throughout the Cold War. The Americans left in 1995 and two years later the RAF took over again, when the Intelligence Corps HQ moved there from Ashford, Kent. It is today the National Defence Intelligence and Security Centre.

Its history began 800 years earlier as a priory of the Gilbertine Order, the only home-grown English religious order, founded by Gilbert of Sempringham in the twelfth century. After the Dissolution of the Monasteries it was acquired in 1538 by the Snowe family, passing in 1576 to Peter Osborn, a colleague of Lord Burghley's (originally spelt Osborne but the 'e' was dropped in the seventeenth century so as not to be muddled with the family of the Dukes of Leeds). The church and one side of the cloisters were demolished, but the principal part of the monastic buildings was converted into a

Chicksands Priory. The Osborn family in the melting snow outside the front door of their Georgianized medieval house.

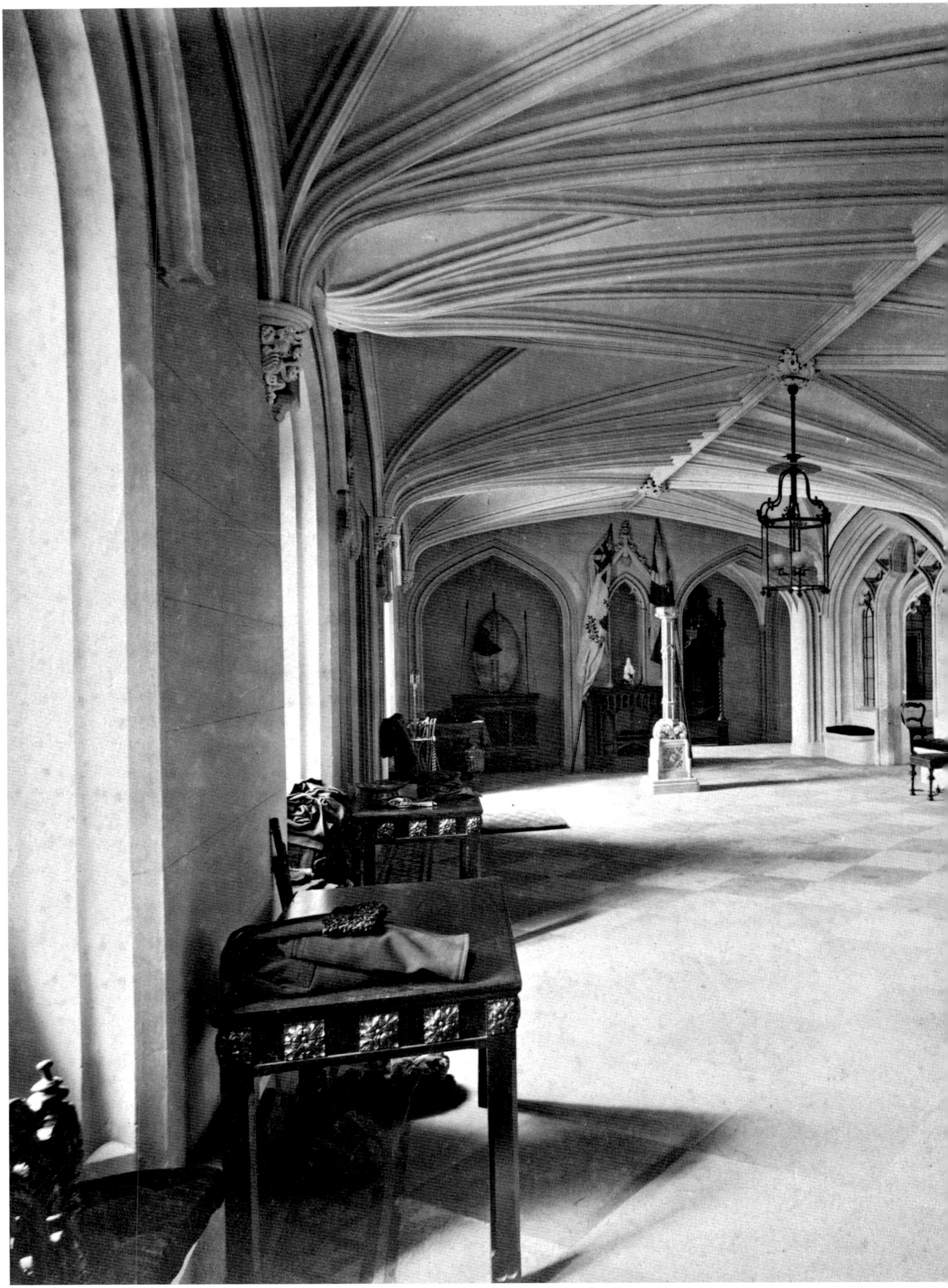

private house, which retained the quadrangular plan of the priory.

The Osborns were Royalists in the Civil War and were created baronets by Charles II as a reward for their loyalty. However, the most interesting historical aspect of the mid-seventeenth century was the story of the love of Dorothy Osborn (1627–95), daughter of Sir Peter Osborn, Royalist Governor of Guernsey, and Peter Temple of a Parliamentarian family. Both families objected, but Dorothy carried on a clandestine correspondence with her betrothed, which was later published and is acclaimed as an historical masterpiece. The letters give a rare insight into life at the time. After the end of the Civil War, both families relented and the couple married in 1665.

The Osborns continued to hold Chicksands until 1935, carrying out improvements from generation to generation; the 3rd and 4th baronets Georgianising the house to the design of Isaac Ware, and landscaping and planting the park; the 6th baronet adding model Victorian estate buildings such as the three Gothic-Revival entrance lodges. Several Osborns also played a role in public life as MPs, generals and admirals. Sir Danvers Osborn, 3rd baronet, was Governor of New York in 1753, but committed suicide. There is a monument to him in Chicksands Wood. Henry Osborn, younger son of Sir Danvers, was Ambassador to the court of Saxony. In his will, he left 100 guineas each to 31 hospitals. His elder brother, Sir George Osborn, 4th baronet, was the chief of the Georgian improvers and employed James Wyatt at Chicksands. In the late nineteenth century Henry, the eldest son of the 6th baronet, was lost at sea following a collision of the steamers *Comtesse de Flandres* and *Princesse Henriette* in the Channel. He too is commemorated in a monument in Chicksands Wood. There are also two obelisks, one celebrating victory in the Napoleonic Wars. These elegies in a rural setting are an idiosyncratic feature of the Chicksands estate: *Et in Arcadia Ego*.

During the First World War Chicksands was run by Beatrice, wife of Sir Algernon Osborn, 7th baronet, as a military hospital for wounded soldiers from the Western Front. The history of Chicksands as a private estate came to an end with the sale by Sir Algernon in 1936. It comprised 2,000 acres and Chicksands Wood (originally called Appeley) covered 300 acres, the largest in Bedfordshire as well as being notable for its family memorials.

The Revd I.D. Parry in *Select Illustrations, Historical and*

✎ *The Entrance Hall with Gothic lierne plaster vault by Francis Bernasconi to James Wyatt's design for Sir George Osborn, 4th baronet.*

⚓ *The Library. This basically Georgian room by Isaac Ware was redecorated in the Victorian period. These rooms are now used as mess to the HQ of the Intelligence corps which occupies the estate.*

✄ *The Gothic landing is also Wyatt's design.*

Topographical of Bedfordshire (1828) wrote in the authentic tone of the Age of Reason: 'The situation of Chicksands judging from the present appearance, was ever a highly pleasing and eligible one. It stands on a slight eminence, with gently rising hills at a short distance behind; along the valley in front flows a brook, formed into a handsome stream, which, in one place, now has a fine artificial cascade; this brook forms one of the sources of the River Ivel. On the hills at the back is a very large and fine wood. The good monks, it appears, well knew how to select for themselves the finest spots and scenery, and to draw together all these objects, which were most calculated to relieve the monotony of their cloistered, and we may truly add, unnatural course of life . . .'

Chicksands was distinguished for its sense of antiquity. The house always retained the character of an adapted monastic structure, which the monks had temporarily vacated. It was also notable for the pretty landscape of the surroundings.

This idyllic landscape is barely recognisable today, although the large wood survives as do some magnificent Oriental planes in the grounds. Chicksands is a military town, with all the tarmac and concrete and wire and street lighting that distinguishes such establishments.

✛ *The antenna erected by the US Air Force in 1962 and demolished after their departure in 1996. It was 120 feet high with diameter of 1,443 feet. Chicksands Wood, covering 300 acres and dotted with poignant family memorials, is the most idiosyncratic surviving feature of the Chicksand estate and is today the backdrop to the Ministry of Defence sprawl.*

Both the RAF and the USAF have built utilitarian housing, distinguishable mainly by the street names. The American brick dreariness is deployed along 'J.F. Kennedy Drive' and 'Truman Place'. The principal military feature was the antenna erected to the west of the priory in 1962 (and dismantled in 1996 following the departure of the Americans). This extraordinary steel structure had a diameter of 1,443 feet and was 120 feet high, like a skeletal Colosseum; it was admired by Pevsner: 'It looks like a C20 super-Stonehenge, or like the elegant steel skeleton of the biggest bull-fighting arena ever.' Its circular outline on the ground is still visible from the air. Otherwise the new buildings in the park are depressingly ordinary. As well as houses, there are schools, a church, shops, a petrol station, gym, leisure centres, a library, sports facilities for rugby, soccer and American football, and fire and police stations. The USAF employed 3,600 people on the site. Today the busy, over-built scene is far removed from the monastic tranquillity of the Gilbertines or the Georgian arcadia of the Osborns.

The priory building, however, survives as the officers' mess and is both a scheduled Ancient Monument and a listed building. Following the departure of the Americans,

it was thoroughly restored in 1997–99. The Georgianised priory is therefore in excellent order but the estate itself has partly disappeared under a rash of military suburbia and security fencing.

✣ *Aerial view of the Chicksands estate today showing RAF housing and social facilities scattered along sprawling tarmac roads.*

Costessey

The Seat of the Jerninghams, Baronets and Lords Stafford, from 1555 to 1935

Costessey is now a suburb of Norwich with a golf course. Its historic owners, the Jerninghams, were a medieval Norfolk knightly family who had remained Catholic after the sixteenth-century Reformation and split of the English church. They lived at Costessey for nearly 400 years, but could trace their ancestry in East Anglia back to the early Middle Ages. Their first recorded ancestor was Hubert Gernegan (the original spelling of the name), who held a knight's fee of the Suffolk Honour of Eye in 1183. The founder of the Costessey (pronounced Cossy) branch of the family was Sir Henry Jerningham (died 1571), eldest son of Sir Edward Jernegan of Somerleyton and Huntingfield, Suffolk. He was one of the first to declare for Queen Mary Tudor (who was then resident at Kenninghall in Norfolk) on the death of Edward VI and raised East Anglia in her support.

She appointed him captain of her guard; he accompanied her from Yarmouth to London for her coronation and defended her from various attempted rebellions. For his loyalty and good service he was knighted, appointed to the Privy Council and made Vice Chamberlain and Master of the Royal Household, and granted several manors in Suffolk and Norfolk, including Costessey in 1555. He rebuilt the Hall in 1564 as an H-plan red brick house in the Tudor style and this remained the seat of the family, little altered into the eighteenth century.

The Jerninghams were created baronets by James I in 1621, but their religion subsequently disbarred them from public life, from royal service or the army in England, and restricted their marriages to other prominent recusant families, including the Throckmortons, Howards, Plowdens, Blounts and Bedingfelds.

❧ The towers of Costessey rising above the trees of a heavily wooded park in 1900. It is now a suburb of Norwich with twentieth-century villas and a golf course.

❧ Grandiose Gothic architecture designed by the antiquarian topographical artist J. C. Buckler, with new Tudor-Gothic wings and a tower to the Hall.

⚓ *An extraordinary amalgam. The Georgianised Elizabethan house on the right, the Catholic chapel designed by Ned Stafford Jerningham and consecrated in 1809 on the left, and J. C. Buckler's neo-feudal eruption in the centre. Two footmen survey the scene.*

In the second half of the eighteenth century, however, their inheritance of the Stafford Howard estates from an elderly female cousin in 1769, and then the gradual relaxation of the penal laws after the 1770s, marked the beginning of an age of renewed prosperity.

The late-Georgian revival of the family fortunes was marked by extensive estate improvements at Costessey. Sir William Jerningham, who inherited in 1774, had been educated in France at the English College at Douai and was a professed Knight of Malta (rare for an eighteenth-century Englishman). As a young man he had served in the Chevaux-Légers de la Maison of Louis XV, as he was prohibited from serving in the English army. After his marriage to Frances Dillon of the Franco-Irish family he settled at Costessey, where like many recusant squires he occupied himself as his own estate manager and increased the rental income by careful direction and improvement. He built a model farm and new stables to the design of John Soane; he also redecorated and modernised the interior of the Hall, but kept its Tudor exterior. Interested in architecture, he himself designed a folly in the form of a Gothic tower in the park at Costessey. With his new plantations, it is shown in the background of his full-length portrait by Philip Reinagle; he holds his design for it, showing the quiet pride he took in his work at Costessey, his architectural embellishments, tree planting and efficient modern farming (his pigs were painted for him by George Morland). He was a good man of business and increased the prosperity of his estates, especially by entrepreneurial development of coal and iron works on the Shropshire estates. The manors of Shifnal and Wrockwardine (part of the Stafford Howard inheritance) were in the East Shropshire coalfield, one of the pioneering areas of the Industrial Revolution near to Coalbrookdale. The increased revenue from mineral royalties on the Midlands estate helped underpin the increasingly neo-feudal, Catholic revival in Norfolk at rural Costessey itself, which was to reach its romantic apogee in the next generation.

George Jerningham, eldest son and heir of Sir William,

married an heiress and her fortune provided a further financial base for the nineteenth-century revival of Costessey. George's younger brother Edward (or Ned), a lawyer, was like their father an amateur architect. He drew up plans to rebuild Stafford Castle (part of the Stafford inheritance, which has always passed down with the title) as a picturesque Gothic folly, which was carried out in 1811. Edward also designed a new private Catholic chapel at Costessey, part inspired by King's College Chapel, Cambridge, with a (plaster) vaulted interior and old Continental stained glass, which enhanced the atmosphere of Catholic piety. It was first used for Sir William's requiem Mass in 1809 and was consecrated the following day.

In 1825, after the completion of complicated legal proceedings, Sir George received a writ of summons as 8th Lord Stafford (a medieval title in fee to which he was the heir general through a convoluted female descent), though he was not to take his seat in the House of Lords until the Emancipation Act of 1829. There were celebrations at Costessey, with church bells and cannon volleys, and a neo-medieval feast with 'one and a half fat bullocks, three sheep roasted, 800 loaves of bread and as many pints of beer

⚓ Sir Henry Jerningham's mid-sixteenth century E-plan house overshadowed by J.C. Buckler's picturesque extensions. The 'Tudor' chimneys are Costessey Ware made from special moulds at the brickworks on the estate, which continued in production throughout the nineteenth century.

as they could consume' for the tenantry. The new peer and his wife had more permanent plans for celebrating the restoration of the barony, with grandiose Gothic architecture designed by the antiquarian topographical artist J.C. Buckler. Work got underway immediately, with the additions of new Tudor-Gothic wings and a tower to the Hall.

Buckler also designed outbuildings on the estates, including a new Catholic church and school at Shifnal in Shropshire, and the laundry and Tudor-style kennels at Costessey for George's son, Henry Valentine Stafford Jerningham, 9th Lord Stafford, in the mid-nineteenth century. The high point of Victorian Costessey was the royal visit of the Prince of Wales (the future King Edward VII) and his new bride, Princess Alexandra of Denmark, in 1866 for which various decorative embellishments

⚓ *The gallery at Costessey by Buckler, furnished as an armoury to form a comfortable Regency vision of the Middle Ages.*

were made by Buckler (who lived to be 90 and was active architecturally to the end). Buckler's work at Costessey was based on detailed study of late-medieval and Tudor architecture in Norfolk, such as Oxburgh and Barsham. The bricks were made on the estate, including terracotta decoration and the tall Tudor patterned chimneys. An offshoot of this was that the estate brickworks became a commercial business producing 'Costessey Ware' throughout the nineteenth century and its chimneys can be found on many Victorian 'Tudor' buildings.

Thereafter Costessey went into rapid decline. Henry Valentine had no children and died, aged 82, in 1884. The estate was inherited by a succession of elderly bachelors. Henry was immediately succeeded by his nephew (the 54-year-old Augustus Stafford Jerningham) as 10th Lord Stafford; he was certified mad. After his death in 1892, he in turn was succeeded by his younger brother, who also did not marry and died in 1913 – the last of the Jerningham Lords Stafford. The title, Shropshire estates, Stafford Castle

and the family portraits, archives and heirlooms were inherited by the heir general Francis Edward Fitzherbert of Swynnerton in Staffordshire (another Catholic recusant dynasty) and have continued to descend in that family.

Costessey and the baronetcy were inherited by the male heir of the Jerninghams, a cousin William Henry (1867–1935), 11th baronet, but he too was a childless bachelor, as was his younger brother. The baronetcy died with the latter's death two years after William Henry, in 1937. So the Jerninghams simply died out with a succession of five elderly unmarried heirs.

The end of Costessey itself can be traced back to the death of the 10th Lord Stafford in 1884, when there were a series of sales of plate books and furniture from the house at Christies. Nevertheless, the Hall and the 3,000-acre estate descended to William Henry in 1913. The empty Hall was, he considered, uninhabitable and four years later, was requisitioned during the First World War and the buildings badly damaged by the regiments of infantry, cavalry and artillery who trained there. Afterwards, it was demolished, *circa* 1925, apart from fragments. It was a notable loss among twentieth-century house demolitions, both for

the original sixteenth-century Hall of the Jerninghams and Buckler's pinnacled and towered extensions, which were the finest example of scholarly and romantic Regency Tudor revival. Even Edward Jerningham's Perpendicular Revival chapel of 1809, with its ancient stained glass (which sold for £17,000), was demolished. The proximity

⚓ The loss of Costessey Hall was notable among twentieth-century house demolitions, both for the original sixteenth-century Hall of the Jerninghams and Buckler's pinnacled and towered extensions, which were the finest example of scholarly and romantic Regency Tudor revival.

✠ *The trees of the park felled and the house in ruin. Like a scene in Prussia after Russian invasion.*

of Costessey to Norwich means that parts of the estate are now embedded in the western suburbs of that city and little remains of Sir Edward's improvements in which he took so much pride in the late eighteenth century, or the romantic ebullitions of the revived Lords Stafford in the nineteenth century.

The park itself is now a golf course – the Costessey Park Golf Club – with bunkers, fairways and greens. The only notable architectural survivor is the belfry block. No trace of the Tudor Hall or Sir John Soane's stables and farm buildings remains. A carved stone chimneypiece and linenfold panelling from the Hall migrated to nearby Hetherscott Hall in the 1920s. Suburban houses encroach on three sides of the park, though some tree planting on the golf course is a reminder of the Georgian landscape, now otherwise lost. Despite its antiquity, Costessey has something of the aura of a theatre set, which rose and fell in a night, leaving hardly a wrack behind.

 The proximity of Costessey to Norwich means that parts of the estate are now embedded in the western suburbs of that city and little remains of Sir Edward's improvements in which he took so much pride in the late eighteenth century, or the romantic ebullitions of the revived Lords Stafford in the nineteenth century.

 Despite its antiquity, Costessey has something of the aura of a theatre set, which rose and fell in a night, leaving hardly a wrack behind.

The Deepdene

A Seat of the Howards from 1483 to 1797, and of the Hopes, from 1807 to 1917

Perhaps as important as the architecture of the Deepdene was the Italianate landscape of the estate with views over Box Hill. It was the *locus classicus* of Italophile gardening in England from the seventeenth to the nineteenth century. Thomas Howard, 14th Earl of Arundel ('The Collector'), had first transformed the setting in the early seventeenth century to make it into that of an Italian *villa*. He planted the evergreen box trees in the vicinity and introduced large edible snails from Italy; their descendants still flourish in the back gardens and allotments of Dorking. The Collector's grandson, the Hon. Charles Howard ('The Alchemist'), a founder member of the Royal Society, continued the Italianate development after the Restoration. He laid out the Amphitheatre, grotto, subterranean tunnel and much tree planting with the advice of the English gardener and diarist John Evelyn, when the latter returned from his Grand Tour of Italy, and also built a laboratory for his chemical experiments. 'The Alchemist' made a special study of the local flora and his 'Herbal' with dried flowers, gathered on the estate in the 1670s, is still preserved fresh and bright in the library at Arundel Castle.

John Aubrey – like Evelyn, a friend of Charles Howard – described the Deepdene and its owner in enthusiastic detail, on visits made between 1673 and the 1690s. Of the house itself he wrote, it 'is not made for Grandeur, but

∽ The Deepdene, Surrey, before demolition in 1967. The central block was the original Georgian house of 1770, remodelled, stuccoed and extended in the 1840s by Thomas Henry Hope who was also responsible for the enormous semi-circular conservatory. A concrete and glass office block described by Pevsner as 'disgraceful and depressing' now overlooks the Dorking bypass which cuts through the park.

∽ The Deepdene, entrance front. The planting on the estate in the 1890s featuring exotic Victorian introductions and banks of rhododendrons. The additional planting was carved out by the Hope family in the 19th-century.

Retirement, (a noble Hermitage) neat, elegant and suitable to the Modesty and Solitude of the Proprietor, A Christian Philosopher . . .'. His descriptions of the garden are well-known and often quoted, and some features he describes can still be discerned, 'the ingeniously contriv'd long *Hope* . . . cast into the Form of a Theatre, on the Sides whereof he hath made several narrow Walks, like the Seats of a Theatre, one above another . . . the Pit . . . stored full of rare Flowers and choice Plants . . .'.

Aubrey also made a sketch of his friend's garden. This shows the 'pit' or level bottom of the 'hope' laid out in ornamental flowerbeds. A short flight of broad steps rose to a central path leading to a plantation of cherry trees. The lower slopes of the steeply rising sides were planted with vines, figs, apricots, quinces, plums, pears and more cherries. At the southern end, the ground rose almost sheer (120 feet) to the terrace with its avenue of trees. Below the terrace on the southern slope was a vineyard covering seven acres. 'From the top of the Hill and the Vineyard,' Aubrey noted, 'is a prospect over Sussex & to Kent & Northwards to Lethered Box hill over the fine valley & W.ward to Hampshire.' Howard's science laboratory is shown on the western side of the hope, or dene, with a parterre in front of it. At the northwest end are marked several 'chambers', a long cave, flowerbeds and a cherry orchard of one and a half acres.

Charles Howard was concerned to consolidate as well as beautify his estate. No records have been traced of his purchase of freeholds in the manor, but the court rolls show he was buying neighbouring copyholds to extend and improve his boundaries. In 1656, he acquired four acres of land called Skeetes, which jutted into his northwestern boundary, and in 1671, he bought from George Rose, blacksmith, 30 acres of copyhold land called Bridhills abutting on the southeastern boundary of the Deepdene. It was on these sunny, well-drained slopes that he planted the vineyard referred to by Aubrey (and later by Defoe), and which produced 'most excellent good wines, and a very great quantity of them'. He pioneered the growing of saffron, a valuable crop, on the Deepdene estate and invented a kiln to dry it; he also experimented with new ways of tanning leather.

Charles Howard's grandson, also Charles, inherited the Dukedom of Norfolk in 1777. The Deepdene remained his favourite residence but was given up by his son in favour of Arundel. He first let it to Sheridan and then sold it to the Burrells who disposed of it to Thomas Hope of the Scottish-Dutch banking family in 1807. It was the Italianate landscape, with its wooded hills, vistas, terraces, grotto, cave and amphitheatre, which so appealed to the Hopes and encouraged them to reconstruct the house in a matching Italianate style.

When Thomas Hope bought the property the house was a dull brick villa designed and built by London surveyor William Gowan for the future 10th Duke of Norfolk in 1769–75. Hope himself was an amateur architect and man of taste, and he employed William Atkinson to execute his own ideas for remodelling and enlarging the house. In 1818–19, he added side wings, a new entrance, offices, stables and a picturesque tower, and stuccoed over the red brickwork. He also built a cyclopean family mausoleum in the grounds in 1819. In 1823, he added an asymmetrical conservatory range to the house. The estate was further extended when he acquired further land eastwards towards Betchworth.

J.P. Neale in 1826 described the Deepdene as 'a spacious mansion of pleasing colour, diversified and varied in its features.' After Hope's death, the house was further remodelled in the 1830s and 1840s by his son, Henry Thomas Hope, who rebuilt the entrance front with twin Italianate towers and transformed the whole place into a magnificent Renaissance *villa-palazzo*, worthy of the Pincio in Rome.

Deepdene was bequeathed to Henry Thomas Hope's wife Anna on his death in 1862. She left the 2,200-acre estate in trust for her grandson Lord Henry Francis Pelham-Clinton (who eventually became 8th Duke of Newcastle), on condition that he added the Hope name and arms, which he did on coming of age in 1887. He never lived at the Deepdene apart from shooting parties and was declared bankrupt for the first time in 1894, when the estate was heavily mortgaged to pay his debts. The house was subsequently let first to Lord William Beresford (a big game hunter) and then to Almeric Paget (MP for Dorking). Meanwhile, Lord Francis Pelham-Clinton-Hope's finances further deteriorated as the mortgages came due for repayment.

In 1912, Deepdene and other properties were placed in receivership. There was a sale of the contents in 1917.

The decision was also taken to sell the estate. In July 1920, the house and 50 acres were sold as one lot for a hotel. Then, in 1921 part of the estate was sold in lots for building development, being conveniently situated on the edge

of Dorking and with a good rail link to London. The Dorking bypass was constructed in the 1930s through the grounds directly in front of the house. News of the sale upset the editor of the 'Estate Market' column in *Country*

⚓ *Looking north down the Deepdene – deep vale – itself, which was originally laid out in the seventeenth century as the spine of the designed Italianate landscape. The Dorking bypass and suburban homes now fill the bottom of this view.*

Life, who wrote on 27 March 1920: 'Historic Associations, even personal and family ties of a fairly intimate character, seem to exercise no restraining influence on the owners of notable properties, and one after another, these pass into the hands of new proprietors and sometimes new uses. Probably not one in a hundred of all who will patronise the new hotel and its type will care a brass farthing about its historical associations.'

Box Hill was acquired in the 1930s by the National Trust for permanent preservation; the lower-lying west parts of the estate, nearest to Dorking, were all developed with spacious suburban housing. In 1939, the house (hotel) and its truncated grounds were acquired under wartime emergency measures as offices by the Southern Railway Company and in 1947, passed to British Rail. With their universal hatred of good architecture, British Rail stripped, subdivided and wrecked the interior. The railway-owned portion of the estate including Betchworth Park Golf Club was sold by the auctioneers Cubitt & West in 1955 and finally, the house was dispatched in December 1967 to Federated Homes Ltd, a development company. They demolished the Hopes' masterpiece in 1969. A large, ugly concrete-and-glass office block by an architectural firm called Scherrer & Hicks was built on the site. Nikolaus Pevsner and Ian Nairn in the *Buildings of England* volume for *Surrey* summed up: 'It is a disgraceful and depressing story.'

But that was not quite the end of the Deepdene. More recently, local enthusiasts have done their best to recover and preserve what remains. A most unlikely discovery is Thomas Hope's neo-Classical mausoleum (1819), which was found buried in the grounds and is now being excavated and restored by the Mausolea & Monuments Trust.

As for the 8th Duke of Newcastle and his hopeless financial mismanagement, he continued to live in a small house on the edge of the Deepdene estate called Harrowlands. On inheriting the ducal seat at Clumber, Nottinghamshire, in 1928, he proceeded to dismember and sell that estate too, and the house there was demolished in 1938, but the park (like Box Hill) was acquired by the National Trust for preservation and public recreation.

☙ *The Deepdene in the guise of a Roman* villa-palazzo, *as rebuilt by Henry Thomas Hope in 1840. It was demolished by British Rail in 1969 and replaced with a modern concrete and glass office block of indescribable mediocrity.*

LEICESTERSHIRE and DERBYSHIRE

3 hours' rail from London, and easy of access for Sheffield, Manchester and the North ;

4½ miles from Kegworth Station on the main line of the Midland Railway; 9 miles from Ashby-de-la-Zouch. Tonge Station is on the Estate.

A Grand Sporting & Residential Domain of 1945 or 4914 Acres.

PARTICULARS, PLAN & CONDITIONS OF SALE

OF THE

FAMOUS FREEHOLD MANORIAL

Sporting and Residential Estate

DISTINGUISHED AS

comprising within its borders some of the most beautiful scenery in the Midlands.   It includes

THE STATELY MANSION,

well known as the Seat of the Marquess of Hastings, and formerly of the Earls of Huntingdon, which occupies a fine situation in a

MAGNIFICENT DEER PARK OF 400 ACRES

BOUNDED BY THE RIVER TRENT;

Most Romantic and Grand Park Scenery ;

The Giant Oaks of hundreds of years growth, the bold undulations formed by three Valleys converging in the Park, and the lovely views from the heights across the Valley of the Trent, are features seldom combined in one estate ;

EXCELLENT COVERT AND PARTRIDGE SHOOTING (about 500 Acres are Woodland)
HUNTING WITH THE QUORN AND MEYNELL

SALMON AND TROUT FISHING

The Mansion, Park, Woodlands, and about

1945 ACRES,

forming a most compact Estate, will be offered in One Lot, or the whole Property of about

4914 ACRES

producing from numerous FARMS, INNS, LIME WORKS, ACCOMMODATION LANDS, &c., a steady

Rent Roll of about £8,000 per Annum,

exclusive of the Mansion, Park, Sporting and Woodlands.

The Manors of Melbourne and Breedon-on-the-Hill, and the Advowsons of Castle Donington and Breedon.

WHICH

HAMPTON & SONS

IN CONJUNCTION WITH

GERMAN & GERMAN

Are instructed by the Trustees of the late Lord Donington to Sell by Auction,

At the Mart, Tokenhouse Yard, London, E.C.,

On THURSDAY, the 24th OCTOBER, 1901,

at TWO o'Clock precisely (unless previously disposed of by Private Treaty).

Donington Park

LEICESTERSHIRE

The Seat of the Hastings Family, Earls of Huntingdon,
Marquesses of Hastings, Lords Donington, from 1464 to 1901

Donington Park is today best known as a motorsport circuit. The race track was created on the southern part of the medieval estate in 1931, during the inter-wars boom of British motor racing. It was requisitioned and used as a military vehicle depot during the Second World War and left derelict thereafter. In 1971, 1,000 acres and the sports circuit were acquired by Tom Wheatcroft, a local construction entrepreneur; the Wheatcrofts still own this part of the estate and are currently attempting to revive the race track after a tenant, Donington Ventures Leisure Ltd, went bankrupt in 2009 as a result of the global financial crash.

Donington Hall itself, a scenic Regency-Gothic pile designed by William Wilkins, and the deer park survive in separate ownership and in 1976 they were bought as the headquarters of British Midlands Airways. British Midlands carried out an ambitious, if not entirely sensitive, restoration of the Hall in the 1980s. They have also built a huge new office block, part concealed in woodland. Eight hundred workers were employed there in 2007, before the recession, but the recent sale to Lufthansa, it is rumoured, may close this office. Various other airlines with names such as Excalibur and Orion also used offices in the grounds so the Donington estate has been a busy place in recent years, unlike most other lost estates, and continued to play a role in the local economy in the late twentieth and first decade of the twenty-first century, though the future looks less confident. The house survives in good structural condition and surprisingly, the ancient deer park is still wild and full of giant oak trees, a wonderful place.

Nevertheless, there has been considerable uglification

since the 1901 sale of the surrounding landscape, a large proportion of which seems to be covered with car parks, gravel extraction, the race track and the airport (situated to the southeast of Donington Hall).

A large modern factory, JWP Computer Services, is situated to the north of the Hall. The Kings Mills site on the Trent, a famous beauty spot in the eighteenth and nineteenth centuries, is occupied by a modern hotel, complete with extensive car parking. To the northeast, an ugly electric power station with two chimneys and huge concrete cooling towers was built in 1954. Following privatisation, this closed and was demolished in 1996. Its site was being developed as a business park intended for light industry and white goods warehouses but much remains empty, like a stretch of moonscape, criss-crossed with optimistic new tarmac access roads and a plethora of unused roundabouts. The little old market town of Castle Donington, whose church spire was a feature of the landscape, is swamped in faceless new housing, five times its size.

The whole area round Castle Donington, with its sprawling and over-leveraged modern development, would make a classic study of the ephemeral boom in the English economy and the collapse after 2007. That is not, however, the point of this book, which is focussed on the earlier history and decline of Donington as an ancient landed estate, the patrimony of an increasingly etiolated medieval dynasty.

Donington was part of the Hastings estates around Ashby-de-la-Zouch in north Leicestershire and originated as a deer park. William Lord Hastings, descended from the Plantagenets, was Lord Chamberlain to Edward IV. The King granted him the Ashby estates in 1464. He converted Ashby Castle into a splendid faux-fortified neo-feudal house in the 1470s, but fell foul of Richard III in 1483 and was subsequently beheaded. In 1529, the Hastings were created Earls of Huntingdon by Henry VIII. Henry, the son

⚭ The sale catalogue of the estate, prepared by Hampton & Sons in 1901. The family fortune was wrecked by the 4th and last Marquess of Hastings, who died destitute and dissipated at the age of 26 in 1868. The 1901 sale was only the delayed last act of that mid-Victorian saga.

⚓ *Donington Hall was a Regency Gothic extravaganza, replete with all the trappings of neo-feudalism. It was designed by William Wilkins in 1793 on the site of a brick house built in the medieval deer park by the Hastings family at the Restoration to replace the castle at Ashby-de-la-Zouch wrecked by the Cromwellians in the Civil War. The house survives, latterly used as the offices of British Midland Airways.*

of the 5th Earl, was leader of the Royalists in Leicestershire during the Civil War and garrisoned Ashby Castle for the King. It fell to the Parliamentarians after a siege in March 1646 and was 'slighted' or deliberately ruined to prevent re-fortification in November 1648. After the end of the Civil War, the Hastings relocated to the medieval deer park at Donington and built a modern redbrick house in a sheltered hollow there, which in turn was replaced by the present grander Regency house.

It passed to the Anglo-Irish Rawdon family as a result of the marriage of John Rawdon, 1st Earl of Moira (1720–93) to the heiress Elizabeth Hastings, 16th Baroness Botreaux, as his third wife (the Huntingdon Earldom went off to another branch of the family). Their son, the 2nd Earl of Moira, was created 1st Marquess of Hastings in 1816. He

commissioned William Wilkins to design the present Gothic mansion at Donington (1790–93), replete with all the trappings of revived feudalism, in celebration of his descent from the Hastings and the Plantagenets. The park was landscaped by the ubiquitous Repton, respecting its ancient deer park character with stagheaded oaks, bracken and splendid views over the Trent to Derbyshire, so that it still looks free of 'the smoothing hands of the great landscapers' (W. G. Hoskins). Repton was responsible for introducing Wilkins as architect of the new house.

A great feature of the Donington estate was the Kings Mills to the north of the park, on the banks of the Trent. These were the oldest and biggest water-powered mills in Leicestershire and had been recorded in the Domesday Book. Over the years, as well as corn they had been used for grinding gypsum, nail making and other industrial purposes. Gothicked at the time of Repton, they were

⚓ *The sale catalogue of the estate, prepared by Hampton & Sons in 1901. The family fortune was wrecked by the 4th and last Marquess of Hastings, who died destitute and dissipated at the age of 26 in 1868. The 1901 sale was only the delayed last act of that mid-Victorian saga.*

Society.—The social advantages of this district must not be overlooked. In the immediate vicinity are many beautiful Seats including—

MELBOURNE HALL	EARL COWPER
CALKE ABBEY	SIR VAUNCEY CREWE, BART.
LOCKINGTON HALL	W. CURZON, ESQ.
COLEORTON HALL	SIR G. H. W. BEAUMONT, BART.
WILLESLEY HALL	THE EARL OF LOUDOUN.
BRETBY PARK	THE EARL OF CARNARVON.
ELVASTON CASTLE	EARL HARRINGTON.
STAUNTON HALL	EARL FERRERS.
BEAUMANOR PARK	MRS. PERRY-HERRICK.
GWITHLAND HALL	EARL OF LANESBOROUGH.
ROTHLEY TEMPLE	F. MERTTENS, ESQ.

"DONINGTON PARK,"

may truly be described as one of

"The Stately Homes of England,"

and few there are which possess the natural charms and picturesque beauty which this property presents. Seated in a

GLORIOUS DEER PARK

of about

400 ACRES,

in which three valleys converge, and adorned on all sides by giant oaks and other forest timber; the views obtained from the Mansion of boldly undulating park land undoubtedly cover some of the most picturesque and romantic park and woodland scenery in the United Kingdom, while from the heights the view across the valley of the Trent is superb. The grand old timber in the park is alone worthy a visit, many of the oaks measuring about 40 ft. in girth at a considerable height above the ground, and there are also magnificently grown beeches, chestnut and other forest timber.

HERDS OF RED AND FALLOW DEER

have unquestionably roamed this park as at present for many hundred years.

"DONINGTON CLIFF,"

on the North-West boundary of the park is well known in the Midlands, the views across the Derbyshire Valley of the Trent are of great extent and striking beauty, it has a sheer fall to the bank of the river, but for the most part is beautifully clothed with timber trees. Close by is a memorial stone called "The Countess' Cross," in the form of a stone cross set on masonry, under which is said to be buried the hand of the Countess of Loudoun.

Another point of interest, just outside the Park is

"KING'S MILL,"

well known throughout the countryside as the most picturesque spot on the River Trent; the massive old stone Mill and Mill-house are of really handsome elevation, although now requiring repair.

Until a few years since a chain of Lakes in the park in full view of the Mansion formed a most pleasing feature, but these were filled by order of the late Lord Donington; at moderate cost these lakes could be

✎ *Donington power station was built in 1954 to improve the view seen on page 88. Recently demolished, it has since been replaced with an unsuccessful business park.*

just the kind of picturesque working element he liked to incorporate in his landscapes and with a heavily wooded cliff behind, they made a perfect picture.

The 1st Marquess, as well as rebuilding Donington Hall and landscaping the estate there, was an enterprising improver of his estates. He promoted the Ashby Canal and created Moira (so-called after his ancestral Irish estate), three miles from Ashby as a new, planned industrial village, with furnaces for smelting the local ironstone, the Moira colliery mining coal and model brick cottages for the workers. At Ashby he developed a new 'genteel and respectable' spa south of the medieval market town with neo-Greek baths (since demolished) and a hotel, exploiting the saline spring water discovered when sinking the colliery shafts at Moira.

But this progressive minded, entrepreneurial streak in the family was overwhelmed by an increasingly arrogant Victorian neo-feudal outlook encouraged by marriages to heiresses, who brought in a multiplicity of titles, including the Scottish Earldom of Loudoun. The decline of the Ashby and Donington estates began in the mid-nineteenth century with the absurd personal extravagance and general uselessness of the 4th and last Marquess: Henry Weysford Charles Plantagenet Rawdon Hastings, who inherited at the age of nine in 1851 and died without a male heir in

1868, aged twenty-six. He broke the family fortune in the five years after coming of age on gambling and racing. As W. G. Hoskins put it: 'The Hastings family were ruined by the fourth Marquess (1842–1868), a jackass of the first order. He ran through a great fortune (horses) and by the age of twenty-six was crawling around on a walking stick.'

The Earldom of Loudoun and the estates passed on his death to his sister Edith, with a quiverful of medieval baronies. After her death, Donington Park passed to her widower, Charles, who had already changed his name to Abney-Hastings. He was created 1st Baron Donington, a title that died out with the death of the 3rd Lord Donington without a son in 1927.

The first Lord Donington was an extremely difficult personality, who fell out with his son and converted to Catholicism. Charles never had the money to maintain the 1st Marquess's grand Regency establishment. He died in 1895. His son, also Charles, who inherited the Earldom of Loudoun from his mother as well as his father's baronetcy, never lived at Donington. This complicated pattern of sidestepping descent, failure of direct male heirs and partible inheritances, was instrumental in the downfall of the Donington Park estate. A more direct male-line descent and some common sense might have saved it.

The fragile nature of the Abney-Hastings pedigree and estates in the Victorian age was not evident from Bateman. He repeated the 1873 figures and misleadingly recorded an estate in 1883 of 32,910 acres worth £37,977 p.a., with 18,638 acres in Ayrshire (Loudoun), 10,174 acres in Leicester and

2,750 acres in Derbyshire (the Ashby and Donington estate). In fact, this seemingly ample patrimony was mortgaged to the hilt. It had been immediately fragmented on Lady Loudoun's death in 1874, when the Ayrshire estates were left sideways to a nephew and much of the peripheral Midlands estate sold to clear debts.

By 1901, when it was finally auctioned off, the Donington Estate was 4,945 acres, with a rent roll of £8,000 p.a. The park was lauded in the sales particulars as a 'Magnificent Deer Park of four hundred acres bounded by the River Trent; most Romantic and Grand Park Scenery; the giant Oaks of hundreds of years growth, the bold undulations formed by three valleys converging in the Park, and the lovely views from the heights across the Valley of the Trent are features seldom combined in one estate.' The 'herds of Red and Fallow deer have unquestionably roamed this park as at present for many hundred years.' They were included in the sale. Much of this heart landscape has survived, though the views out have been much compromised by the twentieth century. W.G. Hoskins in the *Shell Guide to Leicestershire* (1971) was not enthusiastic. Perhaps it was a damp foggy February day, or he had had a bad lunch: 'The view today over the middle Trent valley must include the largest concentration of pylons in England and is of inconceivable dreariness – the Midlands almost at their worst.'

The 1901 sales particulars described the Mills as 'the most picturesque spot on the River Trent'. They were part derelict then and largely burnt down in 1927, but even so Hoskins in 1971 considered them a 'delightful and historic spot'. The present hotel on the site incorporates a remaining bit of the old mills, but is not otherwise something one would want to look at much. The estate was obviously run-down by the time of the sale in 1901. In the particulars the gardens are described as not having received 'much attention recently'. From the Regency glory days, there was a visible decline.

The main part of the property, 'a most compact Estate' amounting to 1945 acres, including the Hall, deer park and woods, was sold privately in June 1902 for £108,000. Both this and the land on the Derbyshire side of the River Trent (which formed the county boundary and ran through the middle of the park), was bought by the Gillies Shields family, who had been Lord Donington's land agents and knew the estate well. Subsequently they made their fortune extracting sand and gravel from the minerals-rich flat fields north of the Trent. They kept the Hall and park until the 1970s, when they sold them in two bits to British Midland and the Wheatcrofts.

Donington Hall was never properly lived in again

⚓ *Donington Park race track.*

as a country house. During the First World War, it was requisitioned for use as a prisoner-of-war camp, being secluded and far from the coast. It is notorious as the only British camp in either World War from which a German prisoner escaped: in 1915, Gunther Plüschow, a German pilot and explorer, escaped from Donington during a storm and made his way to London disguised as a workman. There, he boarded a boat to Holland and got safely home to Munich.

In 1956, after the Russian Communist invasion of Hungary and failure of the Hungarian Uprising, the Gillies Shields made Donington into a refugee camp for displaced Hungarians. They intended to convert it into a refuge for East Europeans, a 'home and school for children of all nationalities who now live without hope in the displaced persons camps in Germany, their parents were our allies, their sufferings caused through loyalty to our cause'. As seen, Donington Hall met a different fate and became an appendage to the East Midlands Airport. It is now German-owned through Lufthansa, as the headquarters of British Midland International.

The Victorian neo-feudal character of the Hastings' estates immediately before their collapse is best summed up by the heraldry-decked monument in the centre of Ashby-de-la-Zouch to Edith Abney-Hastings, Countess of Loudoun. It is a soaring Gothic Eleanor Cross, designed by Gilbert Scott in 1878. Taller than the surrounding houses, it has a resounding dedication: 'Edith Countess of Loudoun, Baroness Loudoun, Tarrinzean, Mauchline, Botreaux, de Moleyns, Hungerford and Hastings. Hereditary Bearer of one of the Golden Spurs'.

Fornham St Genevieve

The Seat of the Kent family from 1731 to 1797 and of the Gilstrap Family from 1842 to 1950

Fornham was an estate developed and embellished (with one ducal interlude) by a series of rich London merchants and bankers. Had it survived, it would have been the ideal property for modern bonus-rich versions of the type, with a potentially fine Wyatt house, prosperous arable farms, partridge shoot and a compact estate village, all with easy train and road access from Bury St Edmunds to the City. Instead, the house was demolished and everything sold after the Second World War. The fringes adjoining Bury are today an industrial estate focussed on the old British Sugar Beet factory. Some of the remainder has been developed as the inevitable 'Eighteen-hole Championship Golf Course' complete with architecturally mediocre red brick hotel and 'spa',

Fornham was a perfect example of a medium-sized 'new' Georgian estate with a good house, neat village, a group of large arable farms, wood, lake and beautifully landscaped park. It was largely the creation of Sir Charles Kent, who inherited in 1760, and employed James Wyatt to remodel the house in the 1770s. At the same time Wyatt was working at Heveningham, also in Suffolk, for another rich city merchant family.

⚓ *Fornham Hall: the staircase. James Wyatt's house incorporated part of an older house situated close to the village of Fornham St Genevieve. The Hall, medieval parish church, outbuildings and Regency stables all formed a cosy architectural group, now mainly demolished (apart from the church).*

advertising itself as 'Leisure is the complete package'. The odd trace of 1940s dereliction still commemorates the wartime requisitioning and military camp, which sounded the death knell of Fornham as a private residential estate.

Fornham in the Middle Ages was part of the large landholdings of the Abbey of Bury St Edmunds. It comprised the ancient manors of Fornham St Genevieve, which belonged to St Edmund from before the Norman Conquest, and Fornham St Martin, which had been attached to the office of Cellarer of St Edmund, and 'Priory', a separate manor assigned to the office of Prior of St Edmund. At the dissolution of the Abbey, one of the richest in England, in 1537, the Fornham lands were granted to Sir Thomas Kytson of nearby Hengrave Hall. He was a Tudor 'new man', a rich mercer and merchant adventurer of the City of London, who was one of the King's executors and beneficiaries.

Fornham was subsequently separated from Hengrave and in the eighteenth century became an independent estate in its own right. It was bought in 1731 by Samuel Kent of Southwark, a grain merchant and distiller. In accordance

with English tradition he used his new mercantile fortune to establish the Kents as a landed family, with their own country seat in East Anglia. He became an MP and High Sheriff of Suffolk – the classic path for Georgian and Victorian new gentry. But Samuel had no son and on his death in 1760, the Fornham estate passed to his daughter and her husband Charles Egleton – a goldsmith of London, who took the Kent name and was created a baronet in 1782.

Sir Charles Kent employed James Wyatt in the 1770s to design a handsome new house, with a plain, dignified exterior and beautifully stuccoed neo-Classical interiors. After his death the estate was bought *circa* 1797 by Bernard Howard of Glossop (q.v.), the heir to the Dukedom of Norfolk. Even after inheriting as 12th Duke in 1815, Bernard Howard kept Fornham as his preferred residence and never moved into Arundel Castle in Sussex, which slumbered under dustsheets, though he greatly extended and expanded the ducal estates there. At Fornham, he enlarged the Kents' house with flanking wings, and elaborate service accommodation, and improved the estate with new stables and sets of ambitious model farm buildings, probably to the design of Robert Abraham, an architectural pupil of

🌲 *The landscaping of the park at Fornham made particularly effective use of cedar trees, always a sign of civilisation. What remains of the park is a golf course, hotel and spa – 'Leisure is the complete package'.*

BURY ST. EDMUNDS

Newmarket 14 miles   Cambridge 27 miles   Ipswich 27 miles   Norwich 41 miles   London 72 miles

Illustrated Particulars, Plans and Conditions of Sale of the

Residential, Agricultural & Sporting Estate

known as

FORNHAM PARK

Georgian Mansion, Park and Grounds
Three Important Farms

Small Holdings.   Accommodation Land
THREE PRIVATE RESIDENCES
60 Cottages and Village Properties
TIMBER
THE WOOLPACK INN

Producing an Actual and Estimated Rent Roll of upwards of

£4,000 per Annum

For Sale by Auction in 52 Lots by

ARTHUR RUTTER, SONS & COMPANY

at THE ATHENAEUM, BURY ST. EDMUNDS
on WEDNESDAY, 25th OCTOBER, 1950
at 11 o'clock

Solicitors :   Messrs. HODGKINSON & BEEVOR, 3, Middlegate, Newark-on-Trent (Tel. No. 761)
Land Agent :   F. KINGSTON SMITH, Esq., Fornham Estate Office, Woodbridge (Tel. No. 14)
Auction Offices : 30, Abbeygate, Bury St. Edmunds (Telephone No. 83)

✠ *The sales particulars prepared by Arthur Rutter & Sons of Bury in 1950 presented Fornham as a traditional Georgian 'residential estate'. But as nearly always in this situation, the house failed to sell and the place was broken up. The Hall was demolished in 1957.*

John Nash and surveyor to the Norfolks' Strand estate in London. (His son, Robert Junior, was sacked for dishonesty from the same position; the duke admonishing him that he had committed the second-worst sin after stealing from widows and orphans – defrauding his employer.)

Fornham was sold following the death of the 12th Duke in 1842. It was bought by William Gilstrap (later baronet and deputy lieutenant), who enlarged it at the peak of the agricultural boom in 1868 by purchasing two thirds of the adjoining parish of Fornham All Saints. He also further extended and altered the house. From Sir William it descended, with progressively declining rent roll, to a grandson: Captain Duncan MacRae.

The estate was requisitioned by the War Department under Defence Regulation 51 in 1939. They installed electricity and their own borehole water supply. A large military camp, with hutments on concrete foundations, was built in the park and at Hall Farm, and the main house was knocked about and neglected. Even the woodland was requisitioned. Surveying all this in 1945, Captain MacRae must have decided there was no future for Fornham and

that the place was a liability. As such, it was typical of the houses and estates given up in the 1950s as a direct result of wartime requisitioning and damage.

At the time of its sale in 1950, the Fornham estate comprised 2,400 acres and was marketed by Arthur Rutter & Co. of Bury St Edmunds as a 'Residential, Agricultural and Sporting Estate'. As well as the 'Georgian mansion', park with lake and fine timber, gardens and glasshouses, there were three 'important farms', several smallholdings, woods, three 'private residences' – the Agent's House, Old Rectory and Hill House – as well as the village with 60 cottages, the Post Office and Woolpack Inn, then bringing in a total income of only £4,000 p.a. Everything was sold in 52 lots at the Athenaeum in Bury St Edmunds. Reading between the lines, the place was in a poor state. Apart from the meagre overall income, there were other hints of wartime damage and neglect as well as general decline – the park was still full of Nissen huts and other military detritus. When properly keepered before the War, the shoot had produced 1,000 to 2,000 pheasants a year in the 1930s but was down to 100 pheasants in 1950. The gardens were neglected and overgrown, the glasshouses derelict.

Captain MacRae's pessimism was reinforced by the fact that the main house failed to sell and it was eventually demolished in 1957, seven years after the surrounding estate was sold off in bits. Ironically, the house could have been easily reduced and improved by demolishing the Regency flanking wings, service block and Victorian excrescences to revive Wyatt's seven-bay centrepiece with elegant semi-circular portico, which with Wyatt's elegant dining room, library and drawing room would have made a delightful house for twentieth-century living, but it was not to be.

Park Farm, comprising 513 acres, and an 'ample Georgian residence' with seven principal and three attic bedrooms as well as an 'exceptional set of Farm premises', all built of brick and flint for the 12th Duke of Norfolk, was sold off as a mini-estate in its own right, with a stud farm and stables. It was successfully re-sold in June 1973 by Jackson-Stops & Staff as a 'First-Class Stud, Arable and Stock Farm', showing how viable the whole estate could have been, had it weathered the war years and their depressing aftermath, but the owner could not foresee the future in 1950.

ॐ *The stables were a characteristically handsome quadrangle of fine brickwork, with a clock cupola.*

✠ *The large walled kitchen garden in wartime, showing the double flower borders planted with cabbages and the glass houses falling into decay.*

⚓ *Hall Farm and Park Farm were splendid examples of Georgian model farms with spacious quadrangles of farm buildings and 'gentlemen's houses' for the prosperous tenants who were the engine of the Industrial Revolution. These buildings were designed by Robert Abraham for Bernard Howard (later 12th Duke of Norfolk), who bought Fornham from the Kents in 1797.*

ℬ *The sun catches the front of Fornham Hall behind a grand cedar tree. The house was demolished in 1957.*

⚓⚓ *The Howard family being driven in a carriage through Glossop in 1905. The houses in the background are in Talbot Road. Twenty years later, after the First World War, the whole estate was sold up, the trees felled, and the Hall after a spell as a nursery school was demolished.*

⚓ *Glossop Hall was a rambling classical house incorporating the Georgian Royle Hall, but was greatly extended to the design of M. E. Hadfield (nephew of the agent) in the 1860s. It was demolished in 1956 after final use as a nursery school. The site is covered with bungalows.*

Glossop Dale

The Property of the Talbot and Howard Families, from 1536 to 1925

Glossop was special among great aristocratic estates in that it was largely industrial. In a bleak and wild corner of Derbyshire, in the Middle Ages Glossop Dale was church property and formed part of the estates of the Abbey of Basingwerke. Then, in the fifteenth century, the manor was leased to the Talbots, Earls of Shrewsbury, who lived at Sheffield Castle, and the 1st Earl appointed his illegitimate son, the Revd Dr John Talbot, rector of the parish of Glossop. At the Dissolution of 1536, the Earls of Shrewsbury gained the freehold as well. They began improvements in the area, including the enclosure of 1,000 acres for sheep farming, with 4,000 sheep, and established the weaving trade for wool cloth. This fledgling industry expanded in the seventeenth century, geared to the nearby Manchester market.

On the death of the 7th Earl of Shrewsbury without a son all his estates, including Glossop, Sheffield and Worksop, passed to his surviving daughter and eventual sole heiress, who married Thomas Howard, 14th Earl of Arundel and eldest grandson of the 4th Duke of Norfolk, in 1604. Thereafter the estate descended in the Howard family. On the death of the 6th Duke of Norfolk in 1684, Glossop was held by his widow for her life and then passed to her daughter Philippa and her husband, Ralph Standish Howard. They were the first members of the family to live at Glossop and built a house there on the banks of the River Royle called Royle Hall (the nucleus of the later Glossop Hall). But their son predeceased them and on Philippa's death in 1731, Glossop reverted to her cousin, the 9th Duke of Norfolk, and the main line of the Howard family.

As a Catholic, the 9th Duke was excluded from public life and so devoted much of his time – he lived to be 90 – to the management of his large estates, in which he took a keen personal interest. He carried out many improvements and new developments. Immediately, he sent to Glossop his northern estate agent from Sheffield to report on the condition of the estate. Vincent Eyre came from an old Derbyshire Catholic family and was a sound businessman: he immediately saw a great future for the local textile industry and made it the estate's policy to encourage this, partly by changing the leases to allow the subdivision of buildings to provide more workshops and other accommodation; also by granting rent rebates in poor years (such as 1757) to enable the tenants to pay for their stocks of wool or thread. Eyre was succeeded on his death in 1759 by his brother Nathaniel and on the latter's death in 1782 by Charles Calvert. All continued the same policy, which led to the rapid economic growth of the area and a dramatic increase in the rent roll, from £3,000 p.a. in the mid-eighteenth century to £11,000 p.a. in the early-nineteenth century. In the 9th Duke's lifetime the population of Glossop increased by 30 per cent, new roads were built and the textile industry changed from wool to cotton. Between 1780 and 1830, 56 mills were built in Glossop.

On the death of the 9th Duke in 1777 the Glossop estate was left to a poor cousin, Henry Howard, whom the Duke had already generously rescued from financial difficulties when Henry's business as a wine merchant failed. This was most important for the future of Glossop because the dukedom of Norfolk was inherited by Henry's son Bernard, who became 12th Duke of Norfolk: Henry Howard divided his time between Sheffield and Royle Hall at Glossop, so that Bernard was partly brought up there, knew and liked the area and continued to take a special interest in the estate. He inherited Glossop from his father before succeeding to Arundel and the dukedom on the death of his cousin Charles in 1815. He too was assisted by a brilliant agent – Matthew Ellison, whom he appointed in 1797 and was the first of a dynasty, who ran the Norfolk northern estate for much of the nineteenth century and were responsible for the economic success of Sheffield and Glossop.

In the late eighteenth century the textile industry began to move from small domestic workshops to large purpose-built mills. Matthew Ellison himself built one of the largest:

⚓ *A unique survival of a Georgian nobleman's warrant with the arms of the 12th Duke of Norfolk over the chemist's shop in Howard Town at Glossop.*

⚓ *To mark his achievement the Duke crowned the station entrance with his crest – a large stone Norfolk lion 'ducally gorged'.*

the Wren Nest Mill. He wrote to a friend in 1814: 'You most probably know that I am resident agent at Glossop about fifteen miles from Manchester, where I have been stationery for the eighteen years of my life and most completely happy, for my employer Mr. Howard [as the 12th Duke was then] is a most amiable man and treats me more as a friend than a servant.' The mastermind behind the management and development of the estates, Ellison repaid the friendship and trust of his ducal employers by making them enormously rich.

The residence of the Howards or their agents at Royle Hall in the eighteenth and early nineteenth centuries had a religious, as well as an economic impact on Glossop. Catholicism had been extinguished in Glossopdale at the Reformation but the Howards reintroduced it, first of all in a private chapel at Royle Hall in the eighteenth century and then in 1803, with a new public parish – All Saints – run

⚓ *The Catholic church of St Charles Borromeo and priest's house designed by Hadfield, and paid for by the 1st Lord Howard of Glossop. It is the burial place of all three Lord Howards of Glossop and their wives.*

by a French emigré priest Fr Barber (3,000 French clergy came to England at the Revolution). At first there was only a temporary church but in 1836, the 12th Duke built at his own expense a splendid new church in the manner of an Italian basilica. This was only one of many improvements for which he was responsible: he planted 50,000 trees annually (beech, larch and Scots pine) and spent nearly £4,000 on improving the roads around Glossop. A leading promoter of the new Turnpike over the Snake Pass in 1821, which greatly improved communications between Manchester, Sheffield and Glossop, he also provided the rapidly expanding town with a well-planned new centre (Howard Town) with a square and impressively designed new Classical town hall on one side (designed by Ellison's nephew, Charles Hadfield). He regularly visited Glossop to inspect progress on the estate, enjoy a little grouse shooting and to admire the surrounding 'mountain' landscape, which was considered the Ideal by early-nineteenth century Picturesque taste.

The 13th Duke (who succeeded in 1842) continued his father's policy towards Glossop, still advised by Ellison. He added the covered market behind the Town Hall in 1844. The Manchester, Sheffield and Lincolnshire Railway Co. refused to build a line to Glossop. Such a line was essential to transport the coal for the steam engines in the mills, so in 1840–45, to save the town from industrial decay, the Duke built the line himself at a cost of £10,000 and marked this achievement with a proud carved stone Howard lion crest over the railway station. In addition to this, he restored the Anglican parish church, rebuilt the rectory and built a school and a Mechanics' Institute. He gave the estate to his second son Edward George, who was created 1st Lord Howard of Glossop in 1869: he rebuilt Royle Hall (renaming it Glossop Hall) and made it his home. During the cotton famine caused by the American Civil War, he borrowed money from the government to set up a public works scheme, building a new reservoir and improved town water supply to provide employment until the cotton industry picked up again. In 1868, he built another Catholic church, St Charles at Hadfield, which combined a double purpose, serving the expanding Catholic population of the area and also intended as a family burial vault for the Lords Howard of Glossop, all of whom are buried there with their wives.

In 1866, Glossop was granted a borough charter and thereafter the Howards were less directly involved in the development and government of the town, though the 1st and 2nd Lords Howard of Glossop continued to give land for parks and public buildings, established a technical

✢ *The railway station at Glossop is dated 1845 by the 13th Duke of Norfolk, who himself paid for building the railway branch line to Glossop – after the railway company had refused to do so – in order to save the cotton industry there.*

college and performed ceremonial duties in the town. According to Bateman in 1883, the estate was 9,108 acres at that time, worth £12,293 p.a.

On the death of the 2nd Lord Howard of Glossop in 1925, the Glossop estate was sold. Bernard, 3rd Lord Howard of Glossop, had unhappy memories of Glossop, where his mother had died young and he had not got on with his stepmother; his younger brother Philip had been killed in the First World War. The black, smoky, industrial atmosphere and wet and gloomy climate in winter made it an unattractive residence. In 1914, Bernard had married Mona Josephine Stapleton, Baroness Beaumont, who had an estate of her own in rich arable Yorkshire and a large historic house, Carlton Towers, of which she was fiercely

⚭ Glossop Hall and Victorian terraced gardens. The private Catholic chapel with Continental looking bell turret is on the right. The grounds became a public park when the estate was sold in 1925.

timber was felled and the estate broken up and resold in bits: the park was acquired by the town council for public recreation and Glossop Hall became a school but was demolished in 1956. The site is covered with bungalows, nicknamed 'Noddy Town'.

Glossop is now a commuter suburb of Manchester: the manufacturing industry has largely gone, the cotton industry having collapsed in the face of eastern competition in the 1930s. Something of the ducal past, though, is maintained in the late-Georgian town centre with the handsome Town Hall, railway station and market hall, all now listed buildings. The park of Royle Hall, however, is irredeemably municipal and the surroundings suburban. The little Victorian entrance lodge has been extended to form a modern dwelling. Overgrazed by too many uncontrolled sheep, the surrounding hills have lost their heather and most of the 12th Duke's ambitious Georgian plantations have been felled without replacement. On a typical damp, gloomy northwestern day, it is all a bit bleak and sad.

proud. When they married, they made a pact that they would live at Carlton and be buried at Glossop, so Glossop went to support Carlton.

The sale of 1925 included 25 farms, grouse moors with grazing rights, quarries and a corn mill, as well as Glossop Hall and the park itself: most of it was bought by a speculative property company. Much of the 12th Duke's

Haggerston Castle

⟡ NORTHUMBERLAND ⟡

The Seat of the Haggerstons (Later Baronets), from *circa* 1200 to 1860,
and of the (Naylor) Leylands until 1938

Haggerston Castle is now a large and popular 'Caravan Holiday Park' on the A1, five miles south of Berwick-on-Tweed, near the Northumberland coast. It was once one of the most historic estates in England, the seat of the Haggerstons of Haggerston for over 600 years, from *circa* 1200 to the mid-nineteenth century, and thereafter of the Leyland family, rich Liverpool bankers, who rebuilt the house and invested heavily in lavish improvements in the Edwardian era. The latter transformed the estate into a progressive Elysium with electricity, special facilities for the workers and developed the *Cupressocyparis leylandii* as a hybrid forest tree.

Haggerston is first mentioned in writing in 1311, when Edward II is recorded as visiting during the Scottish wars. It was then a border pele tower in the middle of a bog; a licence to crenellate was granted by Edward III in 1345, at which time it was described as a 'strong tower'. Its earliest recorded owner was John de Hagardeston, who died in 1210. His grant of land in Northumberland was part of the feudal settlement of England after the Norman Conquest and pacification of the North. In return for defending it against the Scots, he held this boggy tract of ground. The name was anglicised in the fifteenth century to Haggerston: the Haggerstons, like so many of the old Northumberland families – Riddells, Swinburnes, Widdringtons, Selbys,

⟡ Haggerston Castle was rebuilt in 1893–97 and 1908 to the design of Richard Norman Shaw for Christopher John Leyland, who invested a Liverpool fortune in this remote property to make the place a model Edwardian estate. The castle, which had 34 principal bedrooms, was demolished after the Second World War, apart from the Water Tower, and the site is now a caravan park.

⟡ The neo-Classical entrance lodge with fluted Greek columns survived from the previous house built by the Haggerston family, who had lived here since the Middle Ages.

Derwentwaters, even the Percys (until the extinction of the male line in the mid-seventeenth century) – remained Catholic at the Reformation. They were so far away that they felt safe.

When the old pele tower at Haggerston burnt down in 1611, it was rebuilt as a more up-to-date country house by Thomas Haggerston, who was a strong Royalist. He was created a baronet by King Charles I in 1642 in reward for his support in the Civil War. As a recusant Royalist, he was on the wrong side and suffered under the Commonwealth. The Haggerston estate was confiscated by Parliament, but Sir Thomas bought it back in 1652 on payment of a hefty fine.

During the eighteenth century, like other Catholic landowners, the Haggerstons concentrated on managing and improving their property, draining the boggy land to create sheep farms, building gate lodges and cottages, and after the first Emancipation Act in 1778, a small Gothic Catholic chapel in the park for themselves and their tenants. The house itself was rebuilt in plain Georgian style in 1777 and the park landscaped with a lake and plantations.

The senior male line died out with the death of John Haggerston, the 9th baronet, who had succeeded his father in 1858 at the age of six. Haggerston was then sold to the Leylands of Liverpool, whose enormous fortune was derived from the American Caribbean trade, slaves and sugar, and banking. The Haggerston baronetcy continued, however, in the line of a younger son, though the name has changed and the baronetcy has been severed from the Northumberland estate for 150 years.

Thomas Leyland, who bought Haggerston after the death of the 9th baronet, added it to the Leyland settled estates. On his death in 1891, it was inherited by his nephew Christopher John Naylor (1841–1926) of Leighton Hall, Powys. Christopher Naylor changed his name to Leyland. Naylor and Leyland were in fact different spellings of the same name – descendants of two eighteenth-century

⚓ *The stables and motor house were built in 1894 and extended in 1908. They included centrally heated staff accommodation.*

brothers each took one of the different forms, though one descendant who became a baronet eventually squared the circle and became Naylor-Leyland of Nantclwyd (rather like calling oneself Smith-Smith).

Christopher Leyland (as he had become) poured his fortune into improving Haggerston. He rebuilt the house on a vast scale, in 1893–97, with tower, observatory, domed rotunda, ballroom, 34 principal bedrooms, 12 bathrooms, and all the trimmings (it was designed by Richard Norman Shaw). The stables were rebuilt as lavishly as the house in 1894, with garages added for 10 large motorcars in 1908. They were among the most advanced of their date, forming a quadrangle with a bell turret and glazed shelter for washing motors. There was generous accommodation for staff, including eight rooms and two bathrooms for the younger grooms and chauffeurs, and seven semi-detached cottages for the married. The outbuildings included a staff billiard room, staff reading room and 'commodious staff concert hall'. Such generous provision of amenities for their employees was notable even by the standards of paternalist late-Victorian and Edwardian landowners.

The Leylands also provided the estate with its own private electricity supply in the 1890s, one of the earliest in England. A special Electric Light Plant House contained a Parson's Surface Condensor Turbine. There was coal-fired hot water central heating in the main house, outbuildings and staff accommodation. Such advanced domestic technology, with numerous bathrooms, electric light, central heating and motorcars, put Haggerston on a par with the most advanced millionaire estates in America at the time, such as the Vanderbilts' Biltmore in Carolina. This reflected the Naylor-Leylands' Liverpool background, with its close Atlantic and American links, and the interest in progressive industrial technology typical of Lancashire millionaires of the time. All this cosmopolitan splendour made the Edwardian Haggerston estate a very special place.

More conventional improvements were massive tree planting schemes in the surrounding landscape and elaborate formal gardens. The grounds were embellished with a Tea House, Italian Garden, Roman Rose Pergola, sunken Rose Garden, vast rockery, tennis courts and a walled kitchen garden with a 'large double-wing green house'. The American tinge was maintained by a herd of buffalo in the park as part of a private zoo.

Another modern development at Haggerston was the forestry, making use of the hybrid cypress tree *Cupressocyparis leylandii*, originally bred at the Leighton estate in Wales by crossing the Nootka and the Monterey Cypress to produce a hardy, fast-growing evergreen. This triffid-like monster has since grown into a major threat to the English landscape, but in the 1890s was admired as a

⚓ *The Great Hall, with plaster vaulted ceiling, organ and palm trees, was the acme of Edwardian luxury.*

useful tool of modern forestry. C.J. Leyland was given six of the original hybrids from Leighton by his brother and developed them as the 'Haggerston Grey' cypress, useful for screening and filling bleak spots, on this wind-blown coastal estate near the North Sea. After the First World War the Forestry Commission developed the breed with additional hybrids. *Leylandii* is now the biggest-selling item in British garden centres and indeed these hideous, deadening trees account for 10 per cent of all turnover and represent an unwelcome bastard spawn from the original 'Haggerston Grey'.

The glory age of Haggerston with all its modern luxury lasted a bare 20 years and came to an end with the First World War. During the hostilities, the house was occupied by a naval hospital (convenient for the Battle of Jutland, in what was then called the German Ocean, now the North Sea). It was never properly lived in again afterwards. Christopher John Leyland died in 1926 and was succeeded by his son, Captain C.D. Leyland, who had served in the War. He saw no future for Haggerston.

In the presence of a large local crowd Haggerston was sold at the Kings Arms, Berwick in May 1938 by Captain Leyland (the auctioneers were Ward & Price of Scarborough). There were no offers for the estate as a whole and the farms and cottages were therefore disposed of individually. The threat of war (the sale coincided with the Munich crisis), the remoteness of the place and

the over-large scale of the extravagantly enlarged and reconstructed house and outbuildings all combined to doom Haggerston to extinction. Ironically, all the money the Leylands had poured into the place in the 1890s helped mitigate against its survival: it was too rich a Rolls-Royce of a property to appeal to the sort of twentieth-century buyer who wanted a compact estate, a pretty, medium-sized Georgian house and a good shoot. By the 1930s, it had come to seem an anachronistic white elephant.

The auctioneers did their best to push the 'most notable, residential sporting estate, with Historical Associations back to the 14th century', with the magnificent mansion described as 'one of the most imposing masterpieces of modern Architecture and Craftsmanship in the kingdom, an example of the "Italian Renaissance" style'. Looking at old photographs of the gigantic ebullition of Ancaster and Northumberland stone and marble with its slender water tank tower and copper-domed polygonal vestibule, 'Baroque' seems a more appropriate description.

There were five valuable sheep and feeding farms with substantial and well-arranged buildings, grazing lands, the park with ornamental lake and two main entrance drives, the whole village of Fenwick (18 cottages and another Reading Room), the hamlets of Haggerston and New

⚓ *The 'Expansive Ornamental Lake' from the house. It survives as the centrepiece of a colony of 'luxury' holiday lodges or chalets built by Bourne Developments.*

⚓ *The deer park at Haggerston.*

Haggerston, a smithy, a quarry, the Post Office at Beal, the Dower House or shooting lodge, another residence called The Mead, the Chapel and Priest's House plus numerous cottages and the two entrance lodges. Apart from the mansion, everything sold at auction or by private treaty. Haggerston Farm fetched £16,000, Lowlynn Mill Farm £1,200, Brockmill Farm £3,000 and Dairy Farm £7,600. Beal Post Office sold for £410, the cottages from £55 to £205 each, depending on size. Haggerston Quarry was sold to Northumberland County Council for £1,800. The auction brought in a total of £37,000. Properties sold afterwards by private treaty included 'The Mead', with 127 acres for £3,500. Some of the woods and plantations were also sold individually: Marden Plantation, 30 acres of 'well-grown' trees, sold for £475.

As usual, when an estate was broken up there were no offers for the mansion house, which was requisitioned in the Second World War by the military and wrecked in the usual way, with the grounds allowed to fall into dereliction and most of the buildings afterwards demolished. Most of the timber was felled, returning Haggerston to the bleak and wan appearance it had presented before the eighteenth- and nineteenth-century improvements. Alas, pious hopes that the house might become a hotel or school, a hydro or country club did not materialise.

Not much survives architecturally of Haggerston Castle today apart from the now isolated 12-storey water tower and the base of the rotunda (which serves as a 'lounge' for

⚓ *The entrance front with Norman Shaw's porte-cochère and domed rotunda.*

⚘ *The house after fire damage.*

⚘ *Today, the rotunda, which has lost its dome, is used as a 'lounge' by the caravan site.*

⚓ *Haggerston was a military hospital during the First World War.*

⚓ *Surviving fragments – The water tower and the base of the rotunda, and caravans.*

the caravan camp) and the stable block. The chapel is now converted into a private house; the ice house and dovecote also survive, as does an Antelope House in the park, and the framework of the walled Italian garden with a Doric gazebo also still stands. The 'Expansive Ornamental Lake' is surrounded by 'luxury' holiday lodges or chalets built by Bourne Developments; the former gardens and grounds are a dense colony of caravans. With a spa, disco, soccer, cabaret and 'Teen Club', Haggerston is reputedly very popular with northeast footballers.

The fate of Haggerston represents a bit of a falling-off from the progressive and idealistic aspirations of the Reading Rooms and Concert Hall provided by the Leylands for their workforce only 100 years ago, when general literacy in Britain was at an all-time peak of over 90 per cent.

Highhead Castle

IVEGILL, CUMBERLAND

The Seat of the Richmond Family, from the Early Sixteenth Century to 1902, and also of the Hills

The new revised *Pevsner Guide to Cumbria* (2010) by Matthew Hyde captures something of the present character, part-romantic, part-squalid, of this former estate: 'A straight mile of neglected avenue descends gently to [the] grassed over forecourt. Stables to one hand, garden wall to the other, gorgeously elaborate gate piers with Ionic columns ahead. Behind them what was the finest eighteenth-century house in the region . . .'. It is now a collapsing gutted shell. The stables and the former chapel nearby have both been converted to residential use,

while the Home Farm is now the 'High Head Sculpture Valley', of which Hyde notes: 'The effect of indifferent sculpture dotted about the valley – neither wild nor tame, but unkempt – is perilously close to a farmer's junkyard'.

In some ways it is surprising that the Highhead estate lasted as long as it did, as the Richmond family was an exceptionally fragile dynasty. The male line died out in the late seventeenth century. One of the sisters of the last Richmond male heir married Peter Brougham. Their son, Henry Richmond Brougham, took the name on inheriting

☙ *The Georgian castle perched on the edge of a steep wooded ravine. The valley of the River Ivegill formed the centrepiece of the estate and was enhanced by picturesque Georgian tree planting.*

☙ *The forecourt and entrance front of the house built in 1740 by Henry Richmond Brougham. The architect is not known but the design was heavily influenced by James Gibbs.*

⚓ *Looking up the avenue from the house. Stretching for a mile, the avenue is still there but neglected and gap-toothed.*

and built the present splendid house and stables of red Lazonby sandstone in a metropolitan Classical style. His architect is not known, but the design was strongly influenced by James Gibbs. He in turn had no children and the estate once again descended through the female line to a cousin – William Gale, the Whitehaven tobacco merchant – and then through the Richmond-Gale-Braddyll family, who bankrupted themselves building Conishead Priory near Ulverston to the design of Philip Wyatt and sold up there in 1847. With their depleted fortune they tottered on through the nineteenth century at Highhead, but barely maintained the property.

As well as the Georgian architecture, Highhead was notable for its picturesque landscape. The house occupied a naturally defensive and therefore spectacular site on a cliff 100 feet high, overlooking the valley of the River Ive, a romantic raging torrent. The eighteenth-century and early nineteenth-century owners developed these natural advantages to create a superb wooded setting. A walled adjoining kitchen garden was also developed with topiary and terraces, recorded in old *Country Life* photographs but now sadly neglected and overgrown.

The Highhead branch of the Richmond family petered out from the moment the builder of the Georgian house, Henry Richmond Brougham, died childless in 1749 and finally ended at the beginning of the twentieth century. In 1902, the property was bought for £18,000 by Judge Herbert Hills of the International Courts of Appeal in Alexandria, Egypt, who made the house habitable once again and added a neo-Elizabethan servants' wing to the design of J.H. Martindale of Carlisle, but that revival was short-lived. The Hills owned Highhead for three generations (Sir Andrew Ashton Hills died in 1955). Between 1935 and 1950 the house was occupied by Alan Dawes, MP for Penrith (who lost his seat in the election of the latter year); the place was then sold to Gordon Robinson, a Penrith builder, in 1950.

⚓ *Back of the house seen through mature oak trees. The house was gutted by fire in 1956 but survives as a collapsing shell. The estate has been dismembered. Part is used as a park for the display of 'indifferent' modern sculpture.*

⚓ *Looking over the wooded estate landscape from the staircase window, before the fire.*

⚓ *The Ivegill forms a roaring* torrente *in the valley below.*

Robinson was the owner when the house was gutted by fire in 1956 and it has been a ruined shell ever since, though one end continued to be inhabited as a farmhouse and was occupied by Mr Dickman, who bought it after the fire, 'for a very low price'. Demolition consent was sought as recently as 1985, but refused. The estate has been sold in bits and outbuildings have fallen prey to low-grade speculators and conversions. Bits of the shell of the castle have already fallen down.

Highhead Castle is all too remote, too ruined and in too economically depressed an area to be attractive to new money. The almost total collapse of the economy of west Cumberland with the cessation of the tobacco trade, coal and iron industries, in addition to the failure of every government-funded revival project in the course of the twentieth and twenty-first centuries has left places like this beyond recall. The geographical location – not being in Hampshire or the Cotswolds – together with the unattractive character of recent developments, mean that it is unlikely to be snapped up by a prosperous new owner, so the stonework of the house continues to crumble, the trees of the avenue to fall, and the scrub to encroach.

⚓ *The formal garden was embellished with topiary and beds of roses, all gone.*

⚓ *The monumental gate piers remain but the lead sphinxes on top have been stolen.*

⚓ *The stables here have been poorly converted to houses, with unsuitable window joinery.*

Hinton St George

Seat of the Poulett Family, Earls Poulett from 1429 to 1973

After more than 500 years, Hinton St George came to an end because the family was on the brink of extinction, there was no male-line heir and the last Earl Poulett decided to throw in the towel. Indeed, 1968 – the year of Revolutions – was that sort of year when an elderly earl unable to see the future might have thought the world had come to an end. Dissolution started then and everything was sold – lock, stock and barrel – starting with the auctioneers T.G. Lawrence & Son of Crewkerne auctioning off the land in August 1968, followed by the house and its contents in 1973 (after Lord Poulett's death). As always in this kind of mass clearance, there were rich pickings for bargain-hunters.

The house was listed Grade II, so has survived the break-up of the estate and has since been subdivided and converted into several dwellings. That is something: in the 1950s and 1960s, in similar circumstances, it would almost certainly have been demolished. The various residential bits of Hinton House are now graced with their own individual names: Tower House, Wyatt Court, Brettingham Court, and so forth.

The main house at Hinton was of considerable historic interest, if incoherent architecturally. It was a medieval hall house, rebuilt *circa* 1500 and extended in the late sixteenth century. The south front was built *circa* 1630 as a rustic echo of Inigo Jones's Banqueting House and there were several phases of Georgian alterations by good architects: Matthew Brettingham, John Soane, James Wyatt and Jeffry Wyatville.

The Earldom was created in 1706 for John Poulett, 4th

∽ *The once spruce park has lost many trees and has reverted to agriculture. A broken statue of Diana the Huntress succumbs to encroaching vegetation.*

⚐ *The house comprised disparate parts of different dates including a Gothic elevation by James Wyatt with little turrets and battlements, and large subsidiary quadrangles, all facing a well-planted park.*

Lord Poulett, who was First Lord of the Treasury and Lord Steward of the Household under Queen Anne. He was descended from Sir Anthony Poulett, Governor of Jersey and Captain of the Guard to Queen Elizabeth I, whose ancestors had acquired Hinton in 1429. They were Royalists in the Civil War.

In 1883, the Poulett estates in Somerset amounted to a very respectable 22,123 acres, bringing in an income of £21,998. During the Second World War, Hinton House was occupied by St Felix School for Girls from Felixstowe on the threatened east coast. Girls' schools were by far the best wartime tenants of historic houses: they kept the rooms semi-warm and well-ventilated, and were much more appreciative of their setting and well-behaved than boys' schools or urban refugees, let alone soldiers – especially American and Commonwealth soldiers. And so the place came through the War relatively unscathed and the estate benefited afterwards, like other large estates, from the beneficial agricultural climate with its subsidies and fat profits. So the sudden collapse in 1968 was purely personal and family, and not the result of the sort of Gotterdämmerung circumstances to have engulfed other estates recorded in this book.

The descent of the estates in the nineteenth century had not been entirely smooth, however. On the 6th Earl's death in 1899, a dispute arose over the succession. William Turnour Thomas Poulett, who claimed to be the eldest son of the late Earl by his first wife, had indeed been born in wedlock but was never recognised by his father. The inheritance was subsequently contested. Lord Poulett believed William to be another man's son and passed him over for his eldest son by a later marriage. William Poulett claimed the peerage and estates in 1899, but in 1903, the Committee for Privileges disallowed his claim. It was a legal *cause célèbre* as it overturned the presumption that any child born in wedlock was believed to have been fathered by the husband. (Before DNA identification, this was difficult to prove one way or the other.)

The Committee for Privileges instead ruled in favour of the late Earl's son by his third marriage, William John Lydston Poulett, who became the 7th Earl. His son in turn – the 8th Earl – was childless, though also married thrice, and on his death in 1973, all his titles became extinct. He could

❧ The antiquity of Hinton St George was attested by the close manorial proximity of the main house and dependent village, and the medieval church containing five centuries of Poulett family tombs.

⚓ *Part of Wyatville's castellated gatescreen. The entrance to the Stable Court. Magnificent specimen trees once adorned the grounds.*

⚑ *The architectural historian Eileen Harris in front of the west wing at the time of the 1973 sales.*

have left the estate to the descendant of the disputed eldest 'son' of his grandfather, but chose not to. Obviously, there was bitter family feeling and the legal costs of the lawsuit made a dent in the economic viability of the estate. So the dark dramas of a Victorian aristocratic marriage and family inheritance disputes were the background to the collapse of Hinton and the Poulett family, similar to the plot of a nineteenth-century novel by Wilkie Collins. Today, the best memorial to a vanished dynasty is the vast array of family tombs and monuments to the Poulett family in the church of St George at Hinton.

⚑ *The entrance gate with Gribble, Booth & Taylor's 'For Sale' sign in 1973.*

℘ *The park returned to agriculture and cut up with post and wire fences, much of the timber felled.*

Lathom

LANCASHIRE

The Seat of the Stanleys, Earls of Derby, from 1385 to 1702,
and of the Bootle-Wilbrahams, Lords Skelmersdale and Earls of Lathom, from 1724 to 1925

Lathom was one of the most historic estates in the North of England, the major seat of the mighty Stanleys until 1702, and thereafter of the Bootles, who built here the finest Palladian house in Lancashire (since demolished) and employed Repton to landscape the medieval deer park (now ploughed up and treeless). Today, Lathom is a depressing demonstration of Lancastrian indifference: a flat agribus-golferama landscape. It is dominated by Pilkington's Technical Centre, a huge, dull 1950s office block built by the glass-making firm, who acquired the Old Park at that time and demolished Leoni's handsome surviving east service pavilion to make way for it, a notable act of post-war vandalism. The obvious solution – an elegant modern building on the site and to the scale of the old house and incorporating and restoring the two flanking pavilions – was wilfully avoided.

Lathom is a representative example of the almost total abandonment of historic estates in southwest Lancashire in the twentieth century. Each had its own reason – urban pressure, no heirs and extinction and incompetence (or all three) – but the effect is of a comprehensive jumping from sinking ships. Scarisbrick has gone, so too Formby and Rufford, and Wrightington, and Bank Hall and Ince Blundell; also Garswood and Bold. Only Crosby, Knowsley and Meols survive as fully functioning estates, with houses still owned by their hereditary families. In some areas, the houses have survived: Rufford Old Hall as National Trust; Scarisbrick is now a school, Wrightington has become

🐚🐚 *Lathom was the finest Palladian house in Lancashire. On the site of the medieval seat of the Stanleys, Earls of Derby, it was built by Sir Thomas Bootle, Chancellor to Frederick Prince of Wales, to the design of the Anglo-Venetian architect Giacomo Leoni in 1725–40.*

⚓ *The park showing the Coming of Age Party, with a huge marquee, of the 2nd Lord Skelmersdale, later 1st Earl of Lathom, in 1858. This lithograph from the forecourt shows Repton's landscaping of the park; the taller trees were the remains of The Lines, one of the grandest seventeenth-century avenues in England. All the planting was felled when the estate was broken up and sold in 1925.*

a hospital and Ince Blundell is a nursing home run by nuns. However, most have been demolished and generally the whole semi-rural landscape between the M6 and the coast is a textbook example of twentieth-century failure and despoliation – slashed by motorways and dual tracks glowing with orange sodium lighting, depressed by the socially and economically disastrous Liverpool new towns, Skelmersdale and Kirkby, but still interspersed with sad, half-submerged fragments – gate piers, lodges and other once-handsome pieces of architecture. It is a textbook example of what can happen to a whole area when the traditional estate pattern is dissolved, which makes one wonder about the benefits of Town and Country Planning: Lathom can speak for them all.

The early history of the estate is tied up with that of the Stanley family, which is national history. For six centuries they were one of the small circle of governing families and their medieval rise to fame and fortune was spectacular. Originally a small landed family on the Staffordshire-Cheshire border in the twelfth century, they acquired great riches in the fourteenth century when Sir

John Stanley married the heiress Isabel Lathom of Lathom in 1385. She brought her husband far-spreading lands in south Lancashire, including Lathom and Knowsley. From this territorial springboard their descendants acquired political prominence in the fifteenth century, becoming Lords of Man in 1405, Barons Stanley in 1456 and Earls of Derby in 1485 (West Derby in South Lancashire is one of the six Lancashire Hundreds, Saxon territorial divisions). Their withdrawal of support for Richard III was critical in establishing the Tudor dynasty. Stanley loyalty to Henry VII was rewarded with the confiscated estates of Lambert Simnel's Lancashire followers and the 1st Earl's pre-eminence was cemented by marriage (as his second wife) to the King's mother, Margaret Tudor.

The 1st Earl of Derby built a magnificent new house in the centre of the old park at Lathom, which had been enclosed *circa* 1250. It was in the fashionable neo-castle style favoured by leading members of the fifteenth-century nobility, as demonstrated at Hurstmonceux, Tattershall, Ashby-de-la-Zouch and other great seats. Indeed, Lathom was one of the grandest houses of the medieval North. An excavation in 2009 revealed significant traces, under the site of the Georgian house, and showed that the ha-ha reused the

☒ *The Garden Front in a late nineteenth-century photograph.*

☒ *The entrance front and west pavilion. The main block was demolished in 1925.*

medieval moat. A description in an early sixteenth- century poem mentions it as having 'nine towers on high and nine on the outer walls'. Documentary evidence suggests, however, that any turrets were purely symbolic and decorative, and the outer walls had large windows in them. The 1st Earl also built a chantry chapel close by in 1500 and created a New Park with a hunting lodge.

The Derbys were always on the right side in the sixteenth century and acted almost as viceroys in northwest England and the Isle of Man, but their strong attachment to the Royalist cause in the Civil War had tragic consequences for themselves and for Lathom, too. In 1652, the 7th Earl was executed by the Parliamentarians at Bolton and after two heroic sieges when it was proudly defended by the 7th Earl's wife, Charlotte, daughter of

Claude Duke of Tremouille, against General Fairfax, Lathom house was demolished. After the Commonwealth, the 8th and 9th Earls started to build a big classical house with 'a sumptuous and lofty new front' on the medieval site at Lathom. They also transformed the Old Deer Park into a designed landscape with one of the largest and widest avenues in England, over 2½ miles long and 200 yards wide, called The Lines. On the death of the 9th Earl in 1702, the family estates were split, with Lathom going to his daughter, Lady Ashburnham, and Knowsley to his nephew James, the 10th Earl, who rebuilt the old hunting lodge there as the principal Stanley family seat, which it remains. That was the end of the Stanley connection at Lathom, which was sold in 1714 by Lady Ashburnham.

In 1724 it was bought by Sir Thomas Bootle, chancellor

Leoni's garden front. The sympathetically designed attic storey in the centre was added by T. H. Wyatt. The elaborate Victorian formal garden was laid out in the 1860s.

builder of the house, the estate passed to his niece and her husband, Randle Wilbraham, eldest son of the Wilbrahams of Rode in Cheshire. They took the name Bootle-Wilbraham. His son, Edward, was created Lord Skelmersdale in 1828 and his grandson, Earl of Lathom in 1880. The 1st Earl, 'as handsome as he was good and generous', was Lord Chamberlain to Queen Victoria. He built the village school at Lathom and modernised the main block of the Georgian house sympathetically in Leoni's style to the design of T.H. Wyatt. In his lifetime the estates, according to Bateman, comprised 7,213 acres in Lancashire with an income of £21,869 p.a., thanks to the coal revenue from the family colliery at Skelmersdale on the southern edge of the estate.

The collapse of Lathom in the early twentieth century was swift and destructive – and entirely due to the unsatisfactory character of the 3rd and last Earl of Lathom (1895–1930), a theatrically obsessed chum of Noël Coward, who failed to produce an heir and sold up. (The English tended towards two decline and fall default positions: 'horses' or 'boys'.) Before inheriting, he lived at Blythe Hall on the estate, an outlying property near Ormskirk acquired by the 1st Lord Skelmersdale in 1826. *Circa* 1920, he transformed it into an American-style Elizabethan house with a bowling alley and a large Metro-Goldwyn-Mayer classical swimming pool, flashing Doric columns and mosaic work; he plundered Lathom for panelling and marble chimneypieces for the main rooms at Blythe. The gallery of the balcony in the front hall had crystal balusters (though they did not withstand more robust use as a boys' school after the Second World War). Blythe itself survives and is once more a private house. Its enlargement and embellishment was just one of the extravagances that finished off the estate; another was a theatre built for Noël Coward.

In 1925, at the age of 30 the 3rd Earl was forced to sell Lathom to pay off his debts. The destruction was all-embracing: the family archives were fed into the furnaces of the colliery at Skelmersdale. Most of the 3rd Earl's life was spent as a bachelor abroad and at one stage he was ADC to the Governor of Bombay. Three years before his death he unexpectedly married an exotic divorcée, Marie Xenia 'daughter of E.W. Tunzelman, late of Singapore' (as *Burke's Peerage* tactfully puts it), but there were no children.

to Frederick, Prince of Wales; he employed the Anglo-Venetian architect Giacomo Leoni to create a magnificent Palladian house with main block (incorporating the late seventeenth-century shell) and a pair of flanking service pavilions, linked by Ionic colonnades, new stables, lodges and gateways between 1725 and 1740. The park was also embellished with further planting, water features and buildings, including a temple and an icehouse. His successor employed Humphry Repton to re-landscape the Old Park in 1792. Repton's Red Book survives and was in 2004 bought back from America by the Lancashire County Record Office at a Sotheby's sale in New York. It includes his designs for new plantations and a Gothic Dairy, which have now all disappeared.

Under the terms of the will of Sir Thomas Bootle,

✠ *The park was noted for its splendid trees, the product of three centuries of careful planting and landscaping. All were felled after 1925.*

Such was the notoriety of his financial circumstances that the Ritz requested his wedding reception be paid for in advance.

The purchaser of Lathom demolished the main block of the house and felled all the trees in the park. Though the flanking service and stables pavilions were left standing, they were allowed to fall into dereliction, with the east service wing disappearing in the 1950s. Today, only Leoni's west pavilion with the stables survives and, *mirabile dictu*, has recently been well restored and converted to residential use to make a handsome, if poignant memorial of Leoni's work. There is also a gateway with messed-up octagonal lodges and one terrific rusticated gate pier, 20 feet high.

From the Stanley period, the chapel of St John the Evangelist and adjoining almshouses, founded by the 1st Earl of Derby in 1500, survive. It has a charming early nineteenth-century Gothic interior, with Bootle-Wilbraham hatchments and memorial tablets, and bright heraldic glass windows (dated 1823) said to have been designed by a daughter of the house, Mary Charlotte

Bootle-Wilbraham (they were painted by an ancestor of mine: William Seddon). The Stanleys' New Park is now Ormskirk Golf Club and not very medieval-looking.

In recent years, in reaction to all the twentieth-century destruction, there has been a revival of interest in the history of Lathom. The Lathom Park Trust was founded in 2001 and has been the driving force behind the admirable restoration of the stables pavilion and the archaeological study of the medieval deer parks (whose irregular oval boundary outlines are still visible in aerial photographs). Recent excavations supported by the Lathom Park Trust have discovered substantial traces of the medieval Lathom House on the site of the Georgian mansion and show that despite everything, far more historical and archaeological interest survives at Lathom than its ravaged surface appearance might at first glance suggest.

✌ *When the main block was demolished in 1925 the two pavilions flanking the forecourt were left. One originally contained the kitchen offices and the other the stables. After years of dereliction the east kitchen pavilion was demolished by Pilkington the glass manufacturers, in the 1950s.*

⚜ *The kitchen in the demolished east wing.*

Normanton Park

∽ RUTLAND ∽

Seat of the Heathcote Baronets and the Heathcote-Drummond-Willoughbys,
Earls of Ancaster, from 1729 to 1924

The end of the Normanton estate was Wagnerian in its scale and grandeur. It was flooded in 1977 by Anglian Water Authority, pumping water from the Rivers Nene and Welland to create a huge reservoir to supply the Midlands conurbations of Leicester and Peterborough, achieved in the face of much local and national opposition. Farmhouses and cottages were demolished, earth moved and the landscape altered on a scale to completely dwarf the making of the Georgian park in the 1760s. Many people lost their homes and livelihoods in the process. The reservoir is overlooked by the church with Cundy's delightful tower, which was threatened with demolition, but such was the force of opposition that it was saved, strengthened with concrete and left on an artificial headland built out into the water.

Normanton is an example of an estate sold by its owners because it was surplus to requirements. It was part of a large hereditary agglomerate and belonged to a family that found itself with too many properties in the late nineteenth century. In 1883, they owned 163,505 acres (worth £120,900 a year) and were in the very top flight of English landowners. Their chief seats were Grimsthorpe Castle in Lincolnshire, capital of the Willoughby d'Eresby lands (24,696 acres), and Drummond Castle in Scotland, the Drummond property (76,837 acres).

Normanton in Rutland was the inheritance of the Heathcotes and amounted to 13,633 acres. The Heathcote estate also comprised 17,637 acres in Lincolnshire, which were retained. There were also the large Gwydyr Castle estates (30,391 acres) in north Wales. Like many very rich landed families, the Willoughbys started reorganising their estates in the light of political and economic developments in the late nineteenth century and the Gwydyr Castle estate was sold in 1895.

Following the death of Evelyn, Countess of Ancaster, who had occupied it as her dower house since the death of the 1st Earl, in 1910, the Normanton estate (including the villages of Empingham and Edith Weston, and 6,000 acres)

∽ The principal architectural survivor at Normanton is the Georgian estate church, with circular tower inspired by St John Smith Square, London, by Thomas Cundy (junior) in 1826.

∽ The park front of Normanton Hall before demolition in 1925. It was a distinguished Palladian design by Henry Joynes built in 1735–40 for Sir John Heathcote, son of a founder of the Bank of England and Lord Mayor of London.

⚓ *Old photograph of the entrance forecourt with quadrant links and flanking pyramid roofed pavilions added by Kenton Couse (a pupil of Flitcroft) in 1763–67.*

✣ *The garden terrace with Classical statues showing the central bow window added by Thomas Cundy.*

was sold in June 1924. The house itself did not sell – having failed to reach its reserve – and in February 1925, there was a further sale 'of the Fixtures and Fittings in and around the Mansion, which will be sold'. A fire in the summer of that year gutted the building. The shell was demolished at the end of the year and some of the furnishings removed to Grimsthorpe Castle.

The problem with Normanton was that it was too close to the main Ancaster family seat in the adjoining county of Lincolnshire and after the death of the dowager, there was no member of the family to live there. It is strange, though, that the whole place was not bought as a going concern by new money. After all, it was a splendid Georgian house, sensibly sized and conveniently situated, with beautiful interiors, in completely unspoilt landscape in the heart of Midlands hunting territory – the Cottesmore – which was then the height of fashion, with the Prince of Wales and his hangers-on descending on Melton Mowbray every winter. Indeed, it is a mystery why it did not sell *en bloc* to a new owner, like most other large houses in Rutland of the time.

Normanton, with an Elizabethan manor house, had

been acquired in 1729 by the enormously wealthy Sir Gilbert Heathcote (d. 1733), Lord Mayor of London (1711) and one of the founders of the Bank of England. The epitaph on his impressive tomb by Rysbrack, now in Edith Weston Church but formerly at Normanton, describes him as 'a great instrument in founding and well governing the Bank of England'. His son Sir John Heathcote, Bt. rebuilt the Hall in 1735–40 to the design of Henry Joynes, former clerk of works under Vanbrugh at Blenheim. Further sweeping alterations and improvements to the estate were made in the 1760s for Sir Gilbert Heathcote II, Bt. The house was enlarged to the Palladian design of Kenton Couse, a pupil of Henry Flitcroft in 1763–67; the park landscaped at the same time. This involved sweeping away the old village of Normanton to improve the setting. The inhabitants were re-housed in well-built new stone cottages in the estate village at Empingham, described by Pevsner as containing 'many pleasing stone houses and groups of farm buildings'.

✣ *The church was originally built in Classical style for Sir Gilbert Heathcote in 1764 when the old village was moved and the park landscaped. It replaced the medieval village church.*

The 3rd baronet also rebuilt the medieval church in a plain Classical style in 1764. All this made Normanton a *locus classicus* of eighteenth-century estate improvement at its most radical and impressive.

These improvements were carried on for a further generation of Heathcote baronets in the late eighteenth and early nineteenth century, employing Thomas Cundy, father and son (Surveyors to the Grosvenor Estate) as architects. The Cundys made alterations to the house, including the addition of a large central bow window, and enlarged the church in 1794. At the latter, Cundy (junior) rebuilt the lobby and west tower in 1826 as a neo-Baroque design inspired by St John's Smith Square. This delightful structure formed an eye-catcher in the park and remains the principal architectural survivor of the Normanton estate today: still an eye-catcher, though in a radically altered setting.

Cundy (senior) also designed the Home Farm in 1795 for Sir Gilbert Heathcote, his sketch for it surviving in the RIBA Drawings Collection. It formed part of a group of expensive model estate buildings typical of progressive investment in agriculture at the time under the influence of Arthur Young and the Board of Agriculture.

In 1827 occurred the event to determine the long-term future of Normanton. Sir Gilbert Heathcote, 5th baronet (later Lord Aveland), married a great heiress, Clementine Willoughby (later Baroness Willoughby d'Eresby, twenty-third in line to this medieval barony in fee, heritable by females in default of a male heir). She was the heiress of three major ancestral estates: Grimsthorpe Castle from the Dukes of Ancaster, Gwydyr Castle from the Burrells and Drummond Castle from the Drummonds of Perth. All three estates passed to her on the death of her brother, Lord Willoughby d'Eresby, in 1870. Her husband marked his good fortune by changing his name to Heathcote-Drummond-Willoughby.

After Lady Willoughby d'Eresby's death, her son began the rearrangement of this unwieldy assemblage of lands, beginning with the disposal of the Welsh estates in the 1890s and finally, Normanton in 1924–25. Grimsthorpe and Drummond, as well as the large Lincolnshire and Scottish estates, were retained and survive intact in flourishing condition today.

Normanton was sold partly to the farm tenants and much of the timber felled; the church and stables survived. The latter was used to house prisoners-of-war during the

☙ *The church as an eye-catcher in the overgrown park before the landscape was flooded to make a huge reservoir.*

Second World War. W.G. Hoskins, the landscape historian, described the church in the *Shell Guide to Rutland*, in 1964: 'Since the demolition of the great house, the little white church seems to float above a large denuded park.' It still floats but now in a large man-made lake, which actually drowned the estate in 1977.

The revised edition of Pevsner exclaimed: 'How absurd and disproportionate it looks now without its complete base of portico and nave . . . stripped of its dignity, up to its knees in concrete and rubble.' Nevertheless, though the interior has been lost, the tower continues to fulfil its historic function as a beautiful landscape feature. There is still the possibility that it might one day be fully restored, however.

The lake itself (called Rutland Water) is hugely impressive by reason of its scale and careful landscaping in the best 'Capability' Brown tradition, with contoured and irregular banks, also sensitive planting of native trees. Away from the dam, it is now assimilated and looks completely natural. It covers 3,000 acres, is 25 miles in circumference and contains 900 million gallons of water. The lake is stocked with trout, its surface skimmed by pleasure boats and birds. A pair of ospreys hatched at Normanton in 2001, a sign that Nature is prepared to accept it as The Real Thing (assisted by the ministrations of the Trust for Nature Conservation).

The Georgian stables, which survived the demolition of the Hall in 1925 and were used as farmers' barns after the Second World War, overlook the south shore of the lake and have been repaired and converted to a luxury hotel. Though the Hall has gone, and the park and estate are submerged, the surviving shell of the church, the Georgian stables and Cundy's Home Farm at Normanton have found an impressive new landscape setting as architectural ornaments dotting the banks of a vast new lake. It all seems more in the tradition of Georgian estate improvement than the usual messy and careless destruction of the landscape. Indeed, there is something heroic about this kind of death.

⚓ The church today, deliberately preserved as a landscape feature overlooking the vast expanse of water 25 miles in circumference.

Nuttall Temple

NOTTINGHAMSHIRE

Seat of the Sedley Family, *circa* 1719 to 1819, and of the Holden Family, from 1819 to 1927

The destruction of Nuttall Temple after the break-up of the estate in 1927 is one of the half-dozen worst twentieth-century architectural losses among English country houses. It had been built between 1754 and 1757 for Sir Charles Sedley, 2nd baronet, MP for Nottingham, and was designed by Thomas 'Wizard' Wright (1711–86) on the inspiration of Andrea Palladio's Villa Rotonda at Vicenza and Vincenzo Scamozzi's Villa Rocca Pisani. The central, domed octagonal hall had superb Rococo plasterwork by Thomas Roberts of Oxford and ironwork by the Blakewells of Derby. The Sedleys were a scholarly family and as well as a politician, Sir Charles was a Doctor of Civil Law at Oxford. Of Kentish stock, he settled in Nottinghamshire after he married the heiress of Nuttall, Elizabeth Firth, in 1718.

When Sir Charles died in 1778, he left Nuttall to his illegitimate daughter, who married Henry Vernon, a younger son of Lord Vernon of Sudbury, in Derbyshire. In compliance with her father's will, they changed their name to Sedley. The young couple commissioned James Wyatt to design an elegant neo-Classical dining room on the garden front, a complete ensemble down to the chairs and tables, with porphyry scagliola columns and grisaille roundels. The handsome, quadrangular stables with pedimented clock turret too were probably built at this time, though not by Wyatt.

The eldest son lived at Nuttall until he succeeded as Lord Vernon and moved to Sudbury Hall. In 1819, the Nuttall estate was put up for sale, being bought by a family friend, Robert Holden (1766–1844) of Darley Abbey, near Derby, for his younger son. The sales particulars prepared by Mr Robins of Nottingham survive to this day and give a bird's-eye view of a medium-sized Georgian estate. It comprised the Manor of Nuttall, Capital Mansion House, offices, woodlands, cottages and 'the valuable mine of coal under the estate'. There werestables for 20 horses, a Home Farm House and Dairy, Kitchen Garden with 'Extensive grapery' and Melon Ground, an 'Extensive Lawn' park and pleasure ground amounting to some 500 acres with a 'sheet of water' covering 15 acres. In addition, there were sundry cottages, two lodges and another farm of 74 acres, with a 'substantial brick-built farmhouse'.

The coal mine (listed as a great asset in 1819) eventually grew into the nemesis of the place, blighting the

℘ *Gothick seat designed by Thomas 'Wizard' Wright in the form of a sham castle. A good place for a smoke.*

℘ *Nuttall Temple was an English version of Scamozzi's Villa Rocca Pisani in the Veneto. It was part demolished in 1929 and the remains dynamited in 1966, the rubble being used for the M1 motorway through the site.*

The house and park with the lake, photographed by Country Life *in 1923.*

surrounding landscape in the long term. Throughout the nineteenth century the Holdens maintained Nuttall, much as it had been created by the Sedleys. A succession of bachelor brothers succeeded each other as squires, devoting their energies to good works.

In particular, Colonel Robert Holden (the eldest) was 'liberal and tender-hearted', a paragon of Victorian Christian philanthropy: 'One of the rooms of Nuttall Temple was the centre of a system of private outdoor relief which the kind-hearted Squire himself inaugurated and kept up. To this room the poor came for materials to make clothing and not infrequently these gifts were supplemented by articles of food in needy cases . . . If Colonel Holden had had a family to assist him in the enjoyment of the charming estate, it is possible that the bounds of his liberality might have been more circumscribed.'

The last squire was the third brother, the Revd Robert Holden, who inherited the estate in 1913, having been rector of the parish for the previous 35 years in the Georgian and Victorian tradition of younger sons, entering the Church and occupying the family living. Following his death in 1926, the estate was offered for letting or sale as a private residence. Three years earlier, it had been recorded

in *Country Life* with evocative photographs. However, there were no takers for the whole and part of the land and outbuildings were disposed of separately. Eventually, the house itself was sold to a firm of local housebreakers, J.H. Brough & Co. of Beeston, for £800.

In July 1929, after the fittings had been removed, oak props underpinning the mansion were soaked in petrol and set alight. These props were there as a result of mining subsidence, no doubt the reason for the dearth of takers for this wonderful house. For the next 37 years, the central core, too solid for the demolition men, survived as a blasted ruin but provided useful hardcore for the M1 motorway when it was cut through the site in 1966 and the ruins dynamited.

A summerhouse and dovecote dated 1759, the lake, bridge, one gate pier and a cedar tree survive in a blighted landscape on the edge of the creeping Nottingham suburbs to attest to the previous existence, in more civilised times, of a beautiful estate. In 2000, Nuthall Parish Council (the name was changed from Nuttall to Nuthall in the nineteenth century) attached a plaque to the solitary remaining gatepost to commemorate Nuttall Temple and its estate.

Ultimately, the reasons for this terrible debacle were

View from the roof over the lake and park showing the eighteenth-century landscaping of the park, now destroyed.

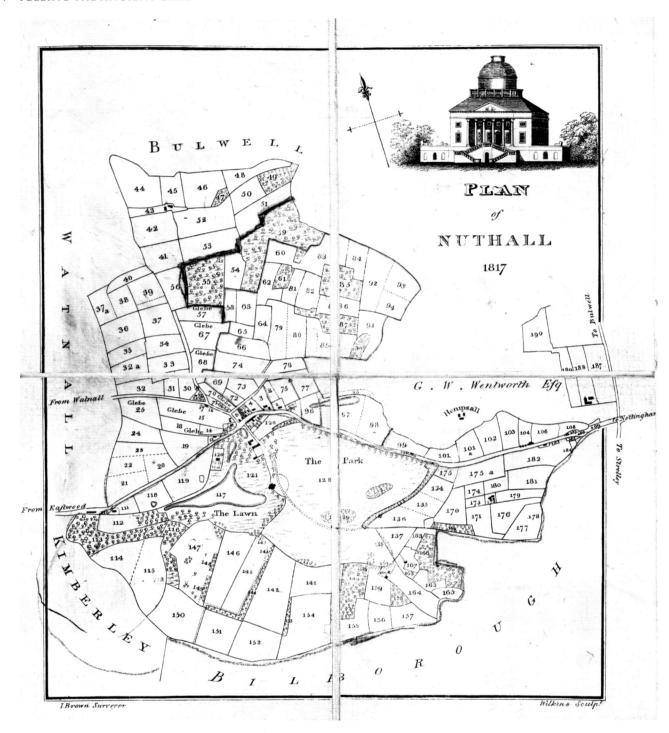

⚓ *Plan of the estate to accompany the sales particulars when Nuttall was sold in 1817 by the Vernon family.*

multifarious: the estate was not large enough to support a substantial house in the twentieth century; the land had been reduced when the Holdens bought the property in 1819; and the surrounding coal mines blighted the area, stunting the trees in the park and undermining the house. In addition to this, a remarkable number of the nineteenth-century squires of Nuttall were bachelors, thus limiting the pool of heirs.

In 1926, Nuttall was inherited by Robert Millington Holden, a cousin: faced with falling rents and death duties, he calculated on the back of an envelope that he would be £1,100 a year better off not living at Nuttall. He did not want to eat into his capital and therefore bought a new, more manageable house at Sibton Castle in the more attractive landscape of Shropshire to replace Nuttall. Until the 1950s, some land was kept at Nuttall but the partial demolition in 1929 marked its demise as an historic estate. In the end, it was a victim of more of the contributors to estate dissolution than most: a small acreage, industrialisation and undermining by coal mines, shortage of direct male heirs and death duties. Its terrible fate as the foundations for a hideous concrete, sodium-lit twentieth-century motorway, however, is worse than a Pugin *Contrast*.

⚜ The Yew Avenue in 1923.

⚜ The entrance front with monumental Corinthian portico in antis, *which gave the house its name of Temple. It was among the half-dozen most serious architectural losses of English country houses in the twentieth century.*

℘℘ *The stables, main entrance and subsidiary village properties before the break-up of the estate in 1927.*

Panshanger

HERTFORDSHIRE

Seat of the Cowper Family, Earls Cowper (and Lady Desborough), from 1720 to 1952

Panshanger was another unnecessary 1950s loss. The seat of the Earls Cowper, it had been inherited by the niece of the childless 7th and last Earl Ettie, Lady Desborough. All three of her sons had been killed: two in the First World War and the third tragically in a car crash in 1926, so there were no male heirs to the Panshanger estate, nor the Desborough estate at Taplow in Buckinghamshire. Following her death in May 1952, Panshanger was sold and the house demolished. Parts of the estate had already been disposed of earlier, in Lady Desborough's lifetime, and the western portion is now covered by Welwyn Garden City, one of the London satellite developments built in the 1920s.

Such a rapid dissolution would have seemed unlikely in the time of the last Earl, who died in 1905, aged 71 and worth over a million pounds. Described as 'a cultivated, agreeable, handsome and capable man', he had served as Lord Lieutenant of Ireland, was a trustee of the National Gallery and Captain of the Gentlemen At Arms. He was also among the richest landowners in England, with 38,000 acres spread through eight counties, including the Cowpers' Panshanger estate in Hertfordshire, then comprising 10,000 acres, and the Wrest Park estate of 9,000 acres, in Bedfordshire. The 7th Earl had inherited Wrest from his mother, Lady Lucas, in her own right and as heiress of the De Grey family, who had owned Wrest since the Middle Ages. This conglomerate landholding produced an income of £60,392 in 1888.

Originally called Cole Green, the Panshanger estate was bought by the 1st Earl Cowper (1665–1723). He came from a family well established in Hertfordshire and Kent. A sound intelligence and the right connections ensured that when he joined the Bar, his legal career was a resounding success, seeing him eventually become Keeper of the Great Seal and Lord Chancellor. In October 1706, he became Baron Cowper of Wingham and was raised to Earl Cowper by George I in 1718. Commensurate with his

Panshanger in the glory days of the last Earl Cowper before the First World War.

The house was a picturesque pile of Regency Gothic design by Samuel Wyatt in 1806 and completed by William Atkinson. It was built on a virgin site chosen by Repton for its scenic appeal.

⚓ *The formal gardens in the time of the 7th Earl in the 1890s were noted for their careful planting and splendour.*

prestige, in 1704 he substantially remodelled Cole Green Park and made further alterations in 1711 to create a house with magnificent interiors, including ceilings by Louis Laguerre. He died in October 1723 after catching a severe cold while travelling from London to Cole Green.

The land of Panshanger itself, north of Cole Green, was added to the estate by the 1st Earl's eldest son in 1719. The splendid collection of pictures, once the glory of Panshanger, was formed by the 3rd Earl, who spent much of his life in Florence, and is now scattered through the museums of the world.

The estate was much enlarged by the 5th Earl Cowper, who built the house on a new site, with better views. The house was a rambling, stuccoed castellated Regency-Gothic building begun by Samuel Wyatt in 1806 and completed by William Atkinson. The great feature was the 'very large and finely timbered park, with the pretty River Mimram running through the midst of it and a truly noble garden', to quote *Country Life*, describing the fully mature

100-year-old landscape in 1898. Begun in 1799, the park was a masterpiece by Humphry Repton and made the most of the valley topography. Repton preserved a number of ancient trees, including the famous Panshanger Oak, and widened the Mimram to create a lake below the house. He himself suggested the site for the new house as the focus of the landscape. Wyatt and Repton were also responsible for the large polygonal walled garden.

The 7th Earl invested large sums in improving his property in the late nineteenth century, building solid white brick and tiled cottages, houses and farm buildings between 1880 and 1899. He maintained Panshanger to the highest standards of Victorian land management – indeed, the woods and gardens were famed for their careful planting and splendour. After his death in 1905, his widow continued at Panshanger until she in turn died in 1913. The first family estate to go was Wrest Park in Bedfordshire: 1,668 acres of which, including the house, grounds, park and woodland and Home Farm were auctioned off in July 1917, one of a group of houses and estates sold during the First World War at a time when prospects were not obviously auspicious. In fact, the prices achieved were

⚓ Pots of hydrangeas in front of the Wyatt-Atkinson house.

quite good, though the house and garden at Wrest did not sell at first. Wrest later became an agricultural college and offices, and the unique garden passed to the Ministry of Works and English Heritage for permanent preservation.

In 1919, Lord and Lady Desborough sold 3,300 acres of the Panshanger estate in 59 lots at the Public Hall in Hatfield. This comprised 12 good farms around Tewin and Digswell, and Digswell House. In the sales particulars prepared by Humbert & Flint, five different sites were designated 'valuable building land'. Digswell House, built in 1807 to the design of Samuel Wyatt – his last architectural work – for the Honourable Spencer Cowper (younger son of the 4th Earl) and its associated land was described as 'a very compact Estate with exceptional advantages for its size. Well-timbered park of 100 acres.' Reference was made to the house's 'imposing elevation' with an Ionic portico and the 'good views'. It sold for £15,000 in 1919, but its days as a private house were numbered. Today, it survives in institutional use on a patch of lawn surrounded by a sea of modern housing. Only one or two cedars stranded along the cul-de-sacs hint at the former existence of a 'well-timbered park'. Ebenezer Howard, the town planner,

bought 1,458 acres in 1919 at a cost of £51,000 for the development of Welwyn Garden City.

The farms also sold well. Digswell Lodge (Lot 25), a farm of 336 acres, sold for £8,000; Tewin Hill Farm (Lot 39) of 311 acres for £6,000, while Coltsfoot Farm (Lot 27) of 176 acres sold for £5,000. The cottages, which were only 30 years old, well-built and in good condition, sold for around £400 each. These were outlying portions of the Panshanger estate and between the wars, the heartland sailed on comfortably enough with the formidable Ettie Desborough as châtelaine and money from the two Cowper Raphael Madonnas sold to the United States for $1.4m to underpin the running costs. Summers were spent at Lord Desborough's Taplow Court overlooking the Thames near Maidenhead, and winters at Panshanger with its excellent pheasant shoot.

Following Lady Desborough's death in 1952, her property was divided between her two surviving daughters. The estate was sold by auction at the Corn Exchange, Hertford in July 1953. It still comprised 3,224 acres, including the

⚓ *An urn carved with Bacchic goats' heads and pan pipes.*
The sculptured embellishments were sold when the house was
demolished in 1958.

house, farms, cottages, allotments and recreation grounds
in the surrounding villages of Tewin, Hertingfordbury,
Birch Green and Cole Green, plus 530 acres of parkland,
bringing in an income of £4,128.17.2d p.a. The auctioneers
were Humbert & Flint and the property was divided into 51
lots for sale, earning a total of £120,000.

Most of the lots were sold, but as usual in this type of
auction of estate, there were no takers for the big house
itself, which lingered on as a white elephant for a few years.
Desperate attempts were made to find an institutional or
educational occupier, but with no success. Finally, it was
sold with 89 acres of grounds to a demolition company
for £17,750 in 1958 and was subsequently demolished for
the break-up value of the materials. The Panshanger Oak
was saved by a preservation order served by the local
authority. Later, the park and surrounding land passed
to La Farge Aggregates for the extraction of sand and

ℬ *The formal terraces round the house were part of Repton's*
comprehensive design for the landscape, begun in 1790 and one of
his masterpieces.

✤ *The formal gardens led imperceptibly into naturalised woodland.*

gravel (much of the surrounding land has since been excavated for this purpose). Strong local opposition and a preservationist campaign have so far prevented the expansion of these destructive works to the heart of the park itself. Remarkably, much of Repton's landscape still survives, even though the house has gone. The fenced-off and decaying shell of the Italianate orangery stands to the west of the visible footprint of the house (demolished 50 years ago), as do the Gothic brick lodges at the entrances to the park.

Pevsner noted: 'All that is left of Panshanger are the remnants of the admirable landscape created after Humphry Repton's plan of 1799. The views from the North of the valley past the trees down to the series of lakes erected by the widening of the river Mimram are still superb, one of Repton's most perfect schemes.' It would make a marvellous site for a new country house on the site so carefully chosen by Repton and the 5th Earl,

which would ensure the perpetuation and rejuvenation of this remarkable landscape. For the moment, however, it remains derelict, with gravel workings eating away at the fringes. It is a depressing end for a great estate laboriously built up on the proceeds of hard work and the profits of the law, beautified and embellished by two centuries of connoisseurship, care, tree planting and investment. Alas, Panshanger died because of a lack of a male heir, as much as from the urban encroachment of the Hertfordshire new towns development.

❧ *Looking towards the house across the valley of the River Mimram, which formed the focus of Repton's landscape. The bones of this still survive despite encircling gravel extraction and Hertfordshire new towns built on estate land.*

⚜ Lady Desborough, last chatelaine of Panshanger, with her husband and elder son at a garden party.

⚘ View over the park and Mimram Valley from the house.

⚘ The Octagonal Dairy with central fountain and cream dishes on a marble shelf, a characteristic Regency model estate building.

⚓⚓ *The Italian Garden with the Orangery. It survived the demolition of the house and still stands in ruinous condition.*

⚓⚓ *Humbert and Flint's sales particulars show the house, garden, entrance gates and Cole Green Avenue in 1953 just before the dispersal and destruction. The Italianate still stands as a ruin.*

By Order of J. J. W. Salmond, Esq., and the Public Trustee.

HERTFORDSHIRE

Hertford 2 miles   Hatfield 4 miles   London 20 miles

Particulars, Plans and Conditions of Sale

OF THE

AGRICULTURAL and SPORTING PROPERTY

KNOWN AS

PANSHANGER ESTATE

extending to about

3,224 acres

FREEHOLD

and comprising

THE MANSION, DAIRY AND MIXED FARMS
RESIDENTIAL PROPERTIES, COTTAGES
ALLOTMENTS, WATERCRESS BEDS, etc.

and about 530 acres of Valuable Woods and Parkland

The let portions producing

PER **£4,128 17 2** ANNUM

FOR SALE BY AUCTION
(unless sold previously)
as a whole or in lots by

HUMBERT & FLINT

at The Corn Exchange, Hertford
on Wednesday, 15th July, 1953, at 11 a.m.

Auctioneers :	Solicitors :
MESSRS. HUMBERT AND FLINT	MESSRS. TROWER, STILL AND KEELING
6 Lincoln's Inn Fields	5 New Square, Lincoln's Inn
London, W.C.2	London, W.C.2
(Tel. CHAncery 3121-5)	(Tel. HOLborn 3613)

Shillinglee Park

SUSSEX

The Seat of the Tournours, Earls of Winterton, *circa* 1660 to 1962

Though the fabric and appearance of Shillinglee was largely Georgian, the estate enjoyed its greatest fame in the nineteenth century as a home to country-house cricket. Both the 4th and 5th Earls of Winterton were first-class cricketers and founders of the Sussex County Cricket Club. At Shillinglee they laid out and maintained a cricket field which was famous in the late-Victorian and Edwardian periods. In the early twentieth century, the great Indian cricketer, Prince Ranjitsinhji, was a guest at Shillinglee every summer for the cricket season.

Such private cricket fields were a notable feature of many estates in the Victorian period. The Duke of Norfolk laid out a beautiful ground in 1894 at Arundel Castle, and the Earl of Sheffield at Sheffield Park at the same time. There was a certain friendly rivalry among Victorian landowners as to the perfection and amenity of their cricket grounds, just as in their splendid new Gothic estate churches.

In the Middle Ages Shillinglee was a satellite estate of the Fitzalans, Earls of Arundel, situated in north Sussex

Shillinglee with the L-shaped Georgian brick house and neat Victorian stables. The house was built in 1735 to the design of Thomas Steel (junior) of Chichester, and extended in 1776 by James Wyatt for the Tournour family.

The house after it was gutted by fire in 1943 during occupation by Canadian troops in the Second World War.

The 5th Earl of Winterton's cricket party on the front steps of Shillinglee. Both the 4th and 5th Earls were first-class cricketers and founders of Sussex County Cricket Club. The private cricket ground was a great feature of the Shillinglee estate. Ranjitsinhji is sitting in the middle of the first row back, to the left of W.G. Grace.

⚓ *The Victorian stables have been converted to a private house as part of the development of the estate by Christopher Buxton, who re-roofed the ruins of the house and converted it to flats in the 1980s.*

near the Surrey border. At the Restoration it was acquired by Sir Edward Tournour, Lord Chief Baron of the Exchequer from 1661–76. It was inherited by his son, Sir Edward Tournour II, whose only offspring, Sara, married Francis Gee. They, too, only had a daughter, Sarah Gee, who married Joseph Garth. Their son in turn, Edward, inherited the estate from his mother in 1744 and changed his name to Tournour. Active in politics, he served as MP for Bramber in Sussex and in 1766, was created Earl of Winterton in the Peerage of Ireland (which did not entitle him to a seat in the United Kingdom House of Lords – Irish peerages were a useful way in the eighteenth century for governments to reward their supporters without clogging up the House of Lords). He died in 1788.

Edward was responsible for developing Shillinglee as a classic Georgian estate, landscaping the park with lake and plantations and building a charming turreted folly – the Deer Tower – walled kitchen garden and other outbuildings. In 1776–78, he employed James Wyatt to add a new south front and remodel the interior of the Palladian house originally built in 1735 to the design of Thomas Steel

(junior), a mason of Chichester. Steel had also designed the Palladian, brick-built Home Farm at the same time and the pedimented entrance lodges at Fisher Street. In harmony with the Georgian ethos, the Victorian earls also built simple brick stables and cottages on the estate.

The 6th Earl of Winterton, born in 1883, lived on into the second half of the twentieth century, dying in 1962. In some ways he was the most distinguished member of the family, with an impressive political career. He sat in the House of Commons for many years, serving as Paymaster General and in other posts, and ended up Father of the House before being given a UK barony and transferring to the House of Lords. He had no children and upon his death, the earldom went to a distant cousin in Canada and the Shillinglee estate was subsequently sold.

The house itself with its beautiful Wyatt interiors was gutted by Canadian soldiers (who accidentally set fire to it during the Second World War, in January 1943) and for many years it was left as a burnt-out shell. Eventually, the core of the estate was converted to a nine-hole golf course: the Shillinglee Park Golf Course. This proved uneconomic and was driven out of business by the glut of larger, more luxurious golf courses developed all over Surrey and north Sussex in the 1980s and 1990s. It was closed in 2002.

In the 1980s, the ruins of the house were bought by

⚓⚓ *Cricketers and spectators at Shillinglee. Prince Ranjitsinhji, the great Indian cricketer, was a guest at Shillinglee every summer for the cricket season. In the top picture the moustachioed cricketer spectating in cap and pads appears to be Lord Hawke. In the lower picture W.G. Grace has borrowed Ranjitsinhji's turban.*

Christopher Buxton, a developer who specialised in the conversion of historic houses to residential use; he converted the stables and outbuildings to individual houses, and has restored and re-roofed the house, converting it to several flats. From the outside, with its re-glazed sash windows and rosy red brick, Shillinglee looks something like its old self. The lake, plantations and walled garden all survive in outline, though not maintained as they were by successive Earls of Winterton. More recently, some of the estate has been purchased by a new owner, who in 2009 was developing it as gallops for horses, with much earth-moving and other new 'landscaping' work, not in keeping with the Georgian landscape. Generally, however, though in many different ownerships, the Shillinglee estate still retains some of its former character and Christopher Buxton's repair and conversion of the main house after war damage means it is still focussed on an attractive Georgian country house.

Thirkleby Hall

Seat of the Frankland Family, Baronets, and the Payne-Gallweys,
Early Seventeenth Century to 1919

Thirkleby is one of the few documented examples of an estate sold as a direct result of the death of the heir in the First World War. It was once the seat of the Franklands, who are first recorded in Yorkshire in the Skipton area, and were at Thirkleby from the early seventeenth century, when William Frankland twice represented Thirsk in Parliament, starting a family tradition which lasted for 200 years. His son, Henry, also represented Thirsk in Parliament and was knighted. Henry's son, Sir William, was created a baronet by Charles II at the Restoration of 1660 and the family continued to represent Thirsk almost as hereditary MPs all through the eighteenth century, just as they had in the seventeenth.

Interesting members of the family in the eighteenth century included Sir Charles Henry Frankland, who was Collector of His Majesty's Customs at Boston, Massachusetts, then Consul General in Lisbon, Portugal, where he was buried for an hour in the ruins following the Lisbon earthquake of 1755, but survived. His brother who succeeded him, Sir Thomas Frankland, had a distinguished naval career and was promoted Admiral of the White.

The Admiral's son, another Sir Thomas (d. 1831), was largely responsible for the character of the estate. He built a new house, stables and triumphal arch gate lodge, all to the design of James Wyatt in his best Classical style, in 1790. All these buildings were distinguished by crisp ashlar masonry (the previous house was Jacobean). At the same time, the park was beautifully landscaped, making especial use of Scots pines and cedar trees.

The *North Riding Directory* of 1899 described Thirkleby as the perfection of a Georgian estate: 'an elegant modern mansion erected by Sir Thomas Frankland Bart in the Italian style from the designs of Mr. James Wyatt,

The last squire, Sir Ralph Payne-Gallwey, in front of Wyatt's Classical house. The death of his son and heir in the First World War precipitated the sale of the estate and demolition of the house in 1927.

architect. It is situated on a gentle eminence in the midst of a spacious well-wooded park. The beautiful avenue of Scotch firs which formed its approach is still a picturesque feature. In the immediate vicinity of the hall are some fine specimens of the cedar of Lebanon, *Wellingtonia gigantea*, and purple beeches. A short distance from the east front is a small artificial lake covering about three acres, and in a wood about 1½ miles distant is a wild duck decoy, both formed about five years ago. The house commands some lovely views of the beautiful scenery around. Towards the East lie the Hambleton Hills and the gigantic form of the White Horse ...'.

As the references to *Wellingtonia gigantea*, purple beech and the duck decoy suggest, planting and estate improvement continued into the nineteenth century, and Thirkleby was a model Victorian estate, as well as a beautiful Georgian one. The son of the builder of the Georgian house inherited a fortune from his Russell cousins and changed his name to Frankland Russell to mark this augmenting of the estates. His wife, Louisa Anne, was the daughter of the Bishop of St David's and as pious as her husband was rich. Following the death of her husband – Sir Robert Frankland Russell, in 1849 – she continued to reign at Thirkleby. Louisa Anne spent her widowhood transforming the estate in accordance with her Tractarian religious principles, rebuilding the parish church of All Saints in the village in memory of her husband in 1851. She chose as her architect Edward Buckton Lamb, one of the Victorian 'Rogue' architects, who worked in a novel version of Decorated Gothic notable for its clashing harmonies. As Pevsner (who had a sneaking admiration for Lamb) wrote: 'The West view cannot easily be forgotten – nor can the East view for that matter. From the West you have the North tower with its disproportionately high spire. It is a veritable riot of forms, perverse and mischievous.'

Thirkleby Church set the pattern for the magnificent estate churches built by Godly and philanthropic

⚜ Wyatt's façade of Thirkleby was purchased by an American in 1927 for re-erection in the United States, but has not been traced to its new home.

Victorian landowners in the North and East Ridings of Yorkshire: from the park at Thirkleby can be seen the even taller spires of the larger and lavish fanes at Baldersby by Butterfield (1856), and Topcliffe by G.T. Andrews (1855) – the gifts of Viscount Downe. Many others followed suit: they are among the architectural glories of the county.

E.B. Lamb was much used by Lady Frankland-Russell, apart from her church. He designed many new buildings on the estate, including the village school and a series of model cottages illustrated in J.C. Loudon's *Encyclopedia* as archetypes for other landowners to follow. Lady Frankland herself designed the stained glass in the stone-vaulted Frankland Chapel, with its designated space for future family memorials that apart from those for herself and her husband have never been filled.

The Frankland-Russells had no son, only daughters, and the baronetcy passed to a male cousin, while the estate descended eventually to their third daughter, who married Sir William Payne-Gallwey. Sir William died in 1881 and was succeeded by his eldest son, Ralph, a leading expert on the crossbow and author of *The Cross-Bow Medieval and Modern, Military and Sporting: Its Construction, History and Management etc.* (1903). His den-workplace in the stables resembled a crossbow museum. The charming, public-spirited quality of Thirkleby in its Victorian and Edwardian heyday was summed up in an inscription on a village water trough erected by Sir Ralph Payne-Gallwey. It read: 'Weary Traveller Bless Sir Ralph who set for thee this welcome trough. 1908'. It was his son who was killed in the First World War, precipitating the sale of the estate and demolition of Wyatt's house.

Naturally, the death of the son and heir came as a terrible blow to his elderly parents. The estate was sold at auction in 1919 but nobody wanted the Hall. It lingered on in deteriorating condition and was eventually sold for demolition in 1927. Wyatt's grand classical frontispiece, with Corinthian columns *in antis*, was bought by an American who took it back for reconstruction in the USA, but it has never been tracked down in its new home.

The site of the house is now a privately owned caravan park with caravans dotted about under the surviving cedar trees and overlooked by Wyatt's handsome stone stables, with their clock cupola. 'A beautiful Yorkshire Caravan park', with private lake and attractive woodlands; 'many caravans are tucked into the edges of the wood whilst others are on the meadows overlooking the beautiful lake' – I dream of bringing Wyatt's house back from the USA and rebuilding it here.

⚜ The entrance front with Victorian billiard room wing and the handsome Georgian stables with tall clock turret on the left. Like the lodge, the stables survive.

⚓ *The triumphal arch entrance gateway was also designed by Wyatt and survived the demolition of the house.*

⚓ Sir Ralph's horse trough in the village with the inscription: 'Weary Traveller Bless Sir Ralph who set for thee this welcome trough 1908'.

⚓ Sir Ralph's den in the stables. He was a noted expert on the crossbow and wrote the standard book on the subject.

⚓ Wyatt's garden front with characteristic domed bow, the plain service wing, and the adjoining stables.

Trentham

The Seat of the Leveson-Gowers, Earls Gower, Marquesses of Stafford
and Dukes of Sutherland, from 1540 to 1919

Trentham in its Victorian heyday was best described by Benjamin Disraeli in his novel *Lothair* (1870) as the lightly fictionalised Brentham: 'And yet it would be difficult to find a fairer scene than Brentham offered, especially in the lustrous effulgence of a glorious English summer. It was an Italian palace of freestone; vast, ornate and in scrupulous condition; and rising itself from statued and stately terraces. At their foot spread a gardened domain of considerable extent, bright with flowers, dim with coverts of rare shrubs, and musical with fountains. Its limits reached a park, with timber such as the Midland counties only can produce. The fallow deer trooped among its ferny solitudes and gigantic oaks; but beyond the waters of the broad and winding lake the scene became more savage, and the eye caught the dark form of the red deer on some jutting mount.'

The Sutherlands were the richest and largest landowners of Victorian Britain – 'Leviathans of Wealth' as the diarist Charles Greville called them. In addition to all their land, they had also inherited half of the Duke of Bridgewater's enormous canal fortune and this provided the capital for the most sweepingly radical estate improvements in early nineteenth-century Britain, of which Trentham was the showpiece.

The sale and break-up of Trentham in 1910–19 was the case of a great Whig family throwing in the towel not because they had run out of money or heirs, but because they were restructuring. In fact, the Sutherlands were still one of the richest families in Britain. The 4th Duke claimed Trentham was uninhabitable because of pollution from the nearby Potteries, with sewage in the River Trent, which ran next to the house. Though Trentham was the Sutherlands' major seat, they had come to associate themselves more with their Scottish title and the huge estates around Dunrobin Castle in Sutherland, preferring the Highlands to the industrial Midlands. The Trentham

∽ Tittensor Chase. The fishing lodge overlooking the pond. Tittensor to the south of Trentham park was the most scenic part of the estate and contained the Victorian dower house surrounded by picturesque gardens and plantations.

∽ Trentham. Engraving of Charles Barry's Italianate palazzo created in the 1830s for the 2nd Duke of Sutherland and his wife, who was Queen Victoria's Mistress of the Robes. The main block retained the early Georgian house remodelled on several occasions.

⚓ *Joseph Pickford of Derby's design for a memorial column. It was not executed.*

estate was 12,000 acres, while the Sutherland estate was over a million acres in 1883.

The 5th Duke (who inherited in 1912) and his advisers completed the dissolution of Trentham and the nearby Lilleshall estate in Shropshire, during and after the First World War, 'owing to pressure of taxation and the heavy death duties on his succession.' Lilleshall House itself, an ugly Jacobean job by Jeffry Wyatville, was sold in 1919 (the family had only ever gone there once a year for Easter). It still stands as a teacher training college. The main part of the Trentham estate was sold in the same year in 560 lots: it fetched a total of £333,000, less than had been invested in it in the nineteenth century under the direction of successive dynamic agents.

The new 5th Duke bought Hampden House in Green Street, Mayfair, a Georgian house by Roger Morris, which remained the Sutherlands' townhouse up to the Second World War. He also acquired picturesque Tudor brick Sutton Place, near Guildford in Surrey as his English country house (more accessible and manageable for the Sutherlands than Trentham when they were not in Scotland or London). Sutton was then considered a gem of Tudor architecture in pretty country, not too far from the capital. So the substitution of Hampden House and Sutton Place for Stafford House and Trentham was also a matter of personal taste; more admired and manageable houses were acquired in place of what then seemed too big, over-rich and elaborate and unfashionable Victorian architecture. The Duke himself admitted: 'I likewise made some readjustments regarding my houses though not so much for financial reasons as for convenience.'

Such a radical break with family history and tradition was also a political gesture against the backdrop of Lloyd George's 'People's Budget', with increased income tax and threat of a land tax, as well as the Parliament Act of 1910 aimed at curbing the House of Lords. This was rightly interpreted as a serious attack on traditional landowners (Lloyd George had claimed it cost as much to keep a duke afloat as a First Class Battleship).

The proceeds of the sales of the Trentham estate in Staffordshire and the first tranche of the Lilleshall estate in Shropshire were invested in the stock market and land in Canada. Though vast, the retained Scottish estates were largely valueless mountain whereas if the Midlands estates had been retained, they would be extremely valuable today. Instead, the house at Trentham was demolished and the farms and cottages sold off individually.

Trentham was monastic in origin. In the Middle Ages, it was a priory of Augustinian canons and was acquired at the Dissolution in 1540 for 1,000 marks by Sir John Leveson, Merchant of the Staple at Calais, who had made his fortune from wool. In the early eighteenth century Trentham was inherited by the Gowers of Stittenham in Yorkshire, who changed their name to Leveson-Gower (pronounced Looson Gore) and made Trentham their principal seat. Their rise to the highest level of the peerage in a century was due to public service but also a spectacular series of marriages to very rich heiresses in successive generations, becoming Barons Gower, Viscounts Trentham, Earls Gower, Marquesses of Stafford and finally, Dukes of Sutherland after marriage to the Countess of Sutherland in her own right, who owned the whole of her eponymous county in the North of Scotland.

The old sixteenth-century manor house at Trentham had been replaced in the early eighteenth century by a

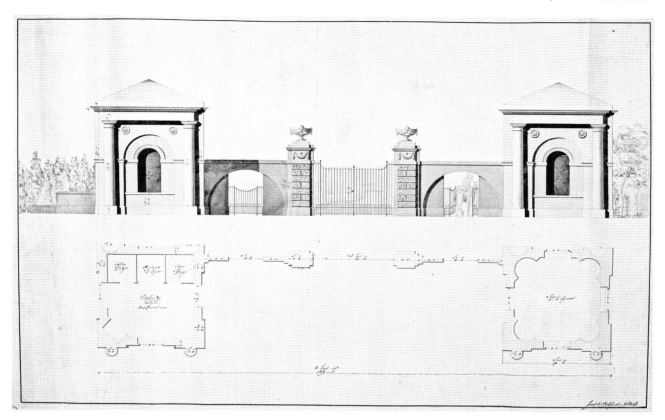

Pickford's design for the lodge gates at the south end of the park, which part survive.

classical brick house by Smith of Warwick on the model of Buckingham House, with formal gardens. This in turn was enlarged, stuccoed and remodelled in 1776 by 'Capability' Brown and his son-in-law, Henry Holland. Brown's work, which began in 1759, also involved landscaping the park and enlarging a 12-acre pond into a magnificent lake by damming the River Trent. Joseph Pickford of Derby designed new lodges and other buildings; Charles Heathcote Tatham designed a mausoleum in 1808. Finally, in the 1830s Sir Charles Barry doubled the size of the house and transformed it into a grand Italianate *palazzo* with tower, porte-cochère and vast formal gardens, comprising terraces and parterre, all reflecting an extravagant love of splendour on the part of the 2nd Duke and Duchess.

The concurrent transformation of the estate was equally spectacular, with large-scale tree planting and near-total rebuilding. Between 1810 and 1820, 37 completely new sets of farm buildings were erected and another eight thoroughly overhauled. The land itself was rearranged to create larger, more practical farms. These included Blurton Waste Farm (1811), Stallington Grange (1811–13), Newstead Farm (1812–13), Knollwall Farm (1814), Blurton Farm (1817), New House Farm (1819), Rough Close Farm, Hanchurch Hill Farm and Little Hales Farm (*circa* 1819). They were mainly designed by John Smith, architect to the Trentham estate from 1805 until his death in 1817 when he was succeeded

by Charles Winks. Winks also designed the monument to the 1st Duke, which stands on a hill to the south of the lake. A column was considered, but thought too like a factory chimney and a giant statue erected instead. William Lewis, estate steward at Trentham, also had a hand in devising the layouts of new farms.

The driving force, however, was the Duke's agent-in-chief based in London, James Loch. Educated at Edinburgh University, Loch was one of a brilliant generation of 'Scotch philosophers' and typical of the new breed of professional land agent. At Trentham he was attempting to put into practice on the largest scale the most advanced and 'enlightened' economic and social theories of the time.

As well as the overall programme of rearranging the land and building new farms, he was also closely involved in all the details of individual new buildings. A letter from him to the Trentham agent in 1817 captures his tone: 'Burlaughton and Hinckes require no observations but to increase the Hinckes cow tyings by two or four . . . Crudgington . . . if the Calf House is too small could you not make an additional one hereafter, at the back like the turnip house? I think the plan otherwise excellent and I trust truly equal to the enlarged farm . . . Woodhouse.

⚘ *The 'black and white' dower house, and grounds at Tittensor Chase. It was retained after the demolition of the main house in 1910 as an occasional ducal residence but sold in July 1914, heralding the dissolution of the whole estate.*

Upon the other side you will see a sketch of Smith's plan as he proposes. I wish you to consider whether mine marked No. 1 would not be less expensive ...'

Loch took great pride in the transformations he masterminded and published them in *Improvements on the Estates of the Marquess of Stafford* (1820). Others found his unquestioning sense of infallibility difficult to take. One critic remarked, 'Surely no one ever dealt so much in superlatives as Mr. Loch does – everything is done with the best intentions, his plans are the best that could have been chosen, the materials used are of the very best quality and the work-people employed are of first-rate abilities.' Nevertheless, these were an important group of neo-Classical farm buildings, of red brick with quadrangular layouts and sleek outlines. Since the sale of the estate they have been allowed to fall into disrepair or been demolished or even altered out of recognition and the landscape part built over. The improvements continued throughout the nineteenth century with model cottages, even an estate railway station.

The main house was demolished in 1910 by the 4th Duke on the grounds sewage from Stoke-on-Trent made it uninhabitable and this left just the porte-cochère, clock turret and some back parts. The top of Barry's Italianate principal tower was bought by the Earl of Harrowby and re-erected in his park at Sandon, a few miles to the south (he had got used to having it in the view and wanted it nearer to home). The dower house at Tittensor was intended to be retained as an occasional ducal residence on the Trentham

estate, but in the end everything was disposed of.

The disposal of Trentham was an heroic act of destruction, probably the largest and most unnecessary sale of a great historic estate in the twentieth century. The situation on the southern edges of the Potteries meant that the moment paternalist ducal ownership and far-sighted professional management were withdrawn much of it was doomed to piecemeal speculative development and spoliation. Between 1911 and 1919, there were no fewer than seven successive sales of land and property. The first – in June 1911, by Knight, Frank & Rutley at the North Stafford Hotel, Stoke-on-Trent – was a seemingly routine sale of 'outlying portions' of the estate, such as often happened and not necessarily the harbinger of total dissolution. It comprised 1,380 acres between Leek and Stone and was made up of four scattered farms, outside the main bloc of the estate, 'all in a capital state of cultivation'. By Midlands' standards, the farms were large, ranging from 100 to 400 acres, with good brick and stone farm buildings.

The next sale – on 28 July 1914, also by Knight, Frank & Rutley – was altogether more sinister since it presaged a change of heart about the whole future and signalled the end of Trentham as a beautifully managed ducal domain. This was the sale of the Tittensor portion of the estate. It formed a solid block of 1,608 acres to the south of the park and included the 546-acre Tittensor Chase, 400 to 600 feet above sea level, and the most picturesque, hilly and wooded part of the ducal property. It was described as 'one of the most beautiful residential estates in England' and included the 'black and white' Victorian dower house – seven reception and 17 bedrooms – built in 1856, together with woodland gardens, rockeries, lily pools, heather valley, tennis lawn and fishponds. The sale included several other substantial 'gentleman's houses'. Altogether, this portion

Barry's Italianate palazzo *and formal garden before demolition in 1910. The place was abandoned because pollution from the Potteries in the adjoining River Trent made the house uninhabitable, though the garden survived in a simplified form for public recreation.*

of the Trentham estate fetched £50,920, including £18,900 for Tittensor Chase itself. Those were very good prices, reflecting the fact that this was high-quality residential property, not purely agricultural. Just over a month later, the First World War broke out and property prices would not reach such levels again until the 1960s.

Once the strategic decision to get rid of the Sutherlands' English estates had been made, it was only a matter of time before the rest of Trentham followed. Encouraged by the wartime rise in farming profits and the illusory consequent increase in land values, the main part of Trentham was dismantled and scattered in consecutive sales lasting two weeks in mid-October 1919. This time the auctioneers were local: Barbers of Wellington in Shropshire. They were among a number of provincial firms of estate agents and auctioneers, who made their names and fortunes in the earlier twentieth century out of the profits from selling historic landed estates, including Bagshaw's of Uttoxeter and Jackson Stops in Northampton. The latter's big break was Stowe in the 1920s, which they sold twice, receiving two lots of commission as the first purchaser immediately put it up for sale again!

The number of lots at Trentham was so enormous that the estate was split into two halves, east and west of the North Staffordshire railway line, each with its own multi-days sale and thick catalogue. They included the Victorian Tudor Revival 'black and white' North Staffordshire Hunt Stables at Trentham and the Regency neo-Classical Kennels with symmetrical façade and crowning cupola, both now

Barber's Sales Particulars in 1919. The auction was an heroic disposal job involving 560 separate lots split into two separate sales.

demolished, as well as all James Loch's ambitious red brick farm houses and buildings; the nineteenth-century ornamental cottages at Ash Green, and the Victorian Trentham Hotel, all then still sprucely maintained and picturesque. The first sale included the principal, west part of the estate, including three entire villages, the main

℥ *The North Staffordshire Hunt Stables.*

℥ *The neo-Classical crescent-shaped Hunt Kennels (demolished).*

℥ *The Trentham Hotel (the only licensed premises on the estate).*

℥ *Properties in Trentham village*

model village at Trentham, and Blurton and Hanchurch, as well as portions of three others: Tittensor, Clayton and Hanford.

Many of the properties were sold to the tenants, including cottages at special low prices, some of the purchasers of which took advantage of this generous paternalist offer to sell on at a hefty profit, as often happened in such situations. The Trentham Hotel was also bought for £11,000 by the tenants, Messrs Joule (it was the only licensed premises on the estate, in line with Victorian philanthropy, which had a strong temperance strain). The Trentham police station was bought for £400 by the village policeman, Sergeant Brandwick, and the vicarage by the vicar.

Aware of the historic moment, Mr Barber gave a good crocodile speech at the opening of the first day, saying it was sad but such properties no longer had a future and it was right that they should be sold off to the many – no doubt mindful of his commission. They were 'about to carry out one of the greatest sales of the United Kingdom involving the break-up of the Trentham Estate, well known

throughout the world.' He added that, 'Every facility had been afforded to tenants to buy, and as he had said they had been handsomely treated.' He hoped the buyers would not take advantage of this generosity to sell on at a profit. Some hope!

Eleven lots amounting to 600 acres were bought by the county council for £24,000 to make small-holdings for the settlement of ex-soldiers on the land under the post-war government scheme: this was a belated example of the Chartist dream of providing people with a few acres and a cow. Such a well-meaning, but crackpot policy foundered on the fact that people wanted well-paid jobs and comfortable suburban homes.

Lady Harriet Granville (sister of the 6th Duke of Devonshire) had once charmingly described the surrounding scrupulously maintained estate landscape of her husband's family in a letter: 'This is in many ways a beautiful place the *tenue*, the neatness, the training of flowers and fruit trees, gates, enclosures, hedges are what in no other country is dreamt of; there is a repose, a *laisser*

✣ *Substantial Georgian and Victorian tenants houses sold to the tenants at special rates in 1919, some of them soon sold on at a profit.*

aller, a freedom, and a security in a *vie de château* that no other offers one. I feel when I set out to walk as if alone in the world – nothing but trees and birds; but then comes the enormous satisfaction of always finding a man dressing a hedge, or a woman in gingham and a black bonnet on her knees picking up weeds, the natural gendarmerie of the country, and most comfortable well-organized country.' With hindsight, this makes sad reading when perusing the sale catalogues of 1919, with their 560 separate lots. The break-up of Trentham was an economic and aesthetic disaster, all the more poignant because enough bits survive to show how wonderful it once was.

Today the road between the park and Trentham village is the ugly, dual-tracked A51. Ash Green is swamped in suburbia, conjoined with the Potteries conurbation. The northeast part of the estate, including Hanford, Blurton and Meir, is solidly built over (and open-cast mined). The charming grounds of the vicarage, which once formed an appropriate backdrop to C.H. Tatham's sombre neo-Classical mausoleum of 1808, are covered with a dreadful 1960s housing scheme. The M6 motorway careers through the former deer park alongside Kingswood. A very large,

modern sewage works covers most of Strangford Farm at the southeast corner of the park, symbolic of Trentham's nemesis.

The loss was not total, however, and against the odds the large Victorian formal parterre and 'Capability' Brown's lake were kept and remained open to the public as a pleasure ground for the people of Stoke-on-Trent, perpetuating the paternalist Victorian tradition. In the 1960s they attracted half a million visitors a year and were only finally sold off by the Sutherland family in the 1980s. They now belong to a private company and have recently been restored by the Dutch gardener Piet Oudolf and are commercially run. A hotel is planned for the site of the house. The grounds recall the glory that once was there, with balustraded terraces and bright formal flower beds overlooking the enormous lake and Capability Brown's hanging woods framing the opposite shore. On a distant hilltop stands the giant bronze statue by Sir Francis Chantrey commemorating the 1st Duke of Sutherland, who surveys the remnants of his largely vanished achievement.

Winestead

Seat of the Hildyard Family from *circa* 1400 to *circa* 1900

As the remote secondary estate of a landed family seated elsewhere, Winestead was the obvious choice for sales and raising of capital for payment of death duties from the end of the nineteenth century onwards. Winestead on the Holderness peninsula to the east of Hull is one of the seemingly most remote places in England.

The Hildyards, who had been settled in the East Riding of Yorkshire since time immemorial, acquired Winestead by marriage at the beginning of the fifteenth century. In 1579, the old manor house was demolished and replaced with a more up-to-date mansion by Sir Christopher Hildyard, Knight, after his only son William drowned as a boy in the medieval moat (the estate was inherited by a cousin). At the end of the seventeenth century, Henry the eldest son became a Catholic and left England for exile on the Continent after the fall of James II. He sold his estate at Winestead to his uncle Sir Robert, who was created a baronet.

The Hildyard house at Winestead was known as the

∾ *The house was demolished in 1936 by Hull Corporation. It was built by Sir Robert Hildyard, 2nd Bt., and is thought to have been designed by Lord Burlington. A hospital was built on the site.*

⚘ *The stables by John Carr of York are dated 1762. They survived the demolition of the Hall and were converted for use as part of Winestead Special School.*

⚜ *The Georgian Hall with the service wing behind. The park had fine trees, nearly all felled by Hull Corporation to make way for new hospital buildings.*

Red Hall to distinguish it from the White Hall, the other large house in the village belonging to the Maisters, leading merchants of Hull. The Red Hall was rebuilt by Sir Robert Hildyard, 2nd baronet in the 1720s but completed by his cousin and heir, also Sir Robert, who had married an heiress. It has been suggested Lord Burlington, whose estate at Londesborough was nearby, may have been involved in the design. It was a well-proportioned, compact, three-storeyed brick building with classically correct pedimented Ionic doorcases on the principal elevations. A smaller block to the north contained the servants' offices.

The handsome stables (dated 1762) were probably designed by John Carr of York, a master of well-arranged classical stable blocks; they have a symmetrical elevation, with two flanking pedimented pavilions, a high central arch and crowning tempietto clock turret similar to those on Carr's stable blocks at Wentworth Woodhouse and Denton Hall, in the West Riding. The stables were a more distinguished work of architecture than the Hall itself, as was sometimes the case in Georgian estates,

demonstrative of the English passion for horses and rural pursuits.

The Hildyard family of Winestead became extinct after ten generations on the death of Sir Robert D'Arcy Hildyard, Bt., who died without male heirs in 1814. He bequeathed his estates to his niece, Ann Catherine Whyte. She married Thomas Blackborne Thoroton of Flintham, Nottinghamshire, and they assumed the name and quartered arms of Hildyard by Royal Licence (their descendants still live at Flintham Hall). They continued to own the Winestead estate and use the Red Hall as an occasional residence, though the Thoroton seat at Flintham became their main base.

The Red Hall was sold to Hull Corporation in the 1890s and demolished in 1936 to make way for Winestead Hospital, which has built ugly brick buildings all over the grounds. Some of the fittings were taken to Flintham. The stable block was retained and is now part of Winestead Special School; the eighteenth-century walled garden and brick and pantiled Keeper's Cottage also survive. With its scattered brick and pantile eighteenth- and nineteenth-century farmhouses and cottages, the village of Winestead still has something of the feel of an estate village. The beautifully restored and maintained twelfth-century

⚓ *Winestead Brickworks. A typical handsome late Georgian estate building making a classical statement with simple means: blank arches and good brickwork.*

church of St Germain contains many memorials to the family from the seventeenth to the nineteenth century, and heraldic hatchments, in the Hildyard Chapel.

Some of the land sold by the Thoroton-Hildyards in the twentieth century was bought by Colonel Rupert Alec-Smith and with the help of the architect Francis Johnson, he converted the Old Rectory into the principal house at Winestead, incorporating fittings from the Red Hall and demolished buildings in Hull (it is now owned by Colonel Alec-Smith's daughter Alex, who maintains it as a perfect example of twentieth-century revived Georgian taste). Winestead is a good example of an estate where, though an ancient family has sold up, their house demolished and its site municipalised, a new estate has been formed and maintains some of the special interest of the place.

Witley Court

The Seat of the Earls of Dudley from 1837 to 1920

Though the house at Witley was stripped and gutted following a fire in 1937, and the estate sold in bits to developers in 1938–39, it was, in this case, not the end of the story. The ruins of the house and the gardens were taken into guardianship by the Department of the Environment in 1972 and are now maintained by English Heritage. The shell of the house has been stabilised as a spectacular ruin, the Victorian parterres and fountains, which were one of the wonders of the Midlands, have been elaborately restored with the help of large grants from the Heritage Lottery Fund and the Wolfson Foundation. Today, the house is a scheduled Ancient Monument, and is listed Grade I; the adjoining church is also listed Grade I and 12 other estate buildings are listed as being of special architectural or historic interest. The gardens and park are included at Grade II in English Heritage's register of Historic Gardens and Landscapes. Such protection has saved what remains from further despoliation.

Witley Court is a heartening example of the statutory protection of historic buildings working in the latter part of the twentieth century: a place that seemed doomed in the 1940s has been saved by post-war preservation laws and a determination that such a magnificent ruin should not disappear altogether. There is hope that further restoration and revival will take place in the future. Nevertheless, the house is gutted and the estate has been broken up, much of the timber felled, the park ploughed up and turned over to utilitarian agriculture (with large modern sheds in sensitive views), the gate-less lodges, walled garden with gardener's house, Home Farm, deer park (the deer shot) and other buildings all sold and converted to bijou private dwellings.

What was once a unified, well-maintained property is now split into numerous different ownerships – the

woodland alone was auctioned in 53 separate lots in 1938. Key structures, including garden ornaments and the Golden Gates, have been removed. Some new houses have also been built here and there. Altogether, this gives the fringes of Witley Court an incongruous ill-maintained, semi-suburban air and despite the heroic efforts of English Heritage, the place will never again look as it did in its Victorian heyday; the bits of the estate cannot be put together again.

Despite the palatial Victorian character, Witley is medieval in origin. In early times it belonged to the Cookseys. In 1655, the estate was bought by Thomas Foley, a very rich iron-master and nail maker from Stourbridge: seven generations of Foleys lived there, all called Thomas. The grandson of the founder was created 1st Lord Foley. He was responsible for the nucleus of the present house. His son, the 2nd Lord Foley, who inherited in 1733, rebuilt the adjoining parish church of St Michael, which he gave the character of an opulent private chapel. The architect was probably James Gibbs. St Michael's Church is the glory of Great Witley and was unaffected by the wreck of the surrounding estate, so has always been well maintained as the local church. It is famous for its baroque decoration, brought in 1747 from the demolished chapel of the Duke of Chandos at Canons, Middlesex, where Handel had been the ducal Kapellmeister. This includes gilded *papier mâché* decoration, stained glass designed by Francesco Sleter and made by Joshua Price, ceiling paintings by Antonio Bellucci and, not least, Lord Foley's spectacular marble monument by Rysbrack. Nowhere else in England is there such a splendid Baroque estate church – it is worthy of Bavaria.

The Foleys were also responsible for creating and landscaping the park with lakes and woods in the eighteenth century, moving the village of Great Witley further away to enhance the views (and to provide better dwellings for the workers). The 3rd Lord Foley, who inherited Witley Court in 1793, employed Humphry

∽ The Georgian chapel of 1747 by James Gibbs, which survived the disintegration of the estate as it served as the local parish church and has always been kept in good condition.

⚓ *The* Perseus and Andromeda Fountain *formed the* pièce de resistance *of the garden, with statuary by Forsyth. When fired the fountain could shoot a jet of water 120 feet into the air,* *with the roar of an express train. Attempts to sell it in the 1930s foundered on its colossal scale and so, happily, it survives.*

shoot a jet of water 120 feet into the air, thanks to Victorian hydraulics and technology.

All this was done by the 1st Earl of Dudley, who expended his good fortune on making Witley into a palace full of art treasures, surrounded by immaculate gardens, a deer park and trim farms. New buildings were erected on the estate. The 2nd Earl, who inherited in 1885, continued the improvements at Witley, including the two main lodges, designed in French Empire style by a local architect, Henry Rowe. He had a distinguished public life, serving as Viceroy of Ireland and Governor General of Australia. An article on the grounds in *Country Life* of 1897 referred to the 'extreme richness' of Great Witley and compared it to Chatsworth and Castle Howard. The place was then still enjoying a golden age of opulence, which lasted until the First World War, with Edward VII and all the smart set coming to stay for huge shooting parties in the winter.

The eldest son, Viscount Ednam, who served in the 10th Hussars after Oxford, was killed in the opening battle of the First World War, in 1914. The 2nd Earl's younger brother, Gerald Ward, was in the Life Guards and was also killed in the same year. In 1920, Lady Dudley was drowned, swimming in the sea near their Irish house. This concentration of tragic deaths, combined with a fall in revenue from the family's industrial empire in the Black Country, and the generally changed circumstances after 1918 was the backdrop to Lord Dudley's decision to sell the Great Witley estate and retrench to Himley Hall, the old Ward family home which had replaced Dudley Castle as their main residence in the eighteenth century. Himley was a large Regency house, which had been extended to the design of William Atkinson.

Between the Wars, the Himley estate continued to be kept up in smartest style. The 2nd Earl remarried in 1924, his second wife being the beautiful film actress, Maureen Swanson. They were friends of the Prince of Wales (Edward VIII) and other members of the Royal Family, including the Duke and Duchess of Kent. Edward VIII spent his last house party before the Abdication at Himley. With the outbreak of the Second World War, Himley was requisitioned and sold afterwards for offices to the National Coal Board, which had taken over all the nationalised Dudley coal mines. It now belongs to Dudley Council, which runs it as a country park and corporate

Repton to design formal terraces around the house and added heroic Ionic porticos on both fronts to the design of John Nash in 1805. His general extravagance, however, combined with his brother and heir's excessive gambling and general uselessness, wrecked the Foley fortune. In 1837, the family was forced to sell off the whole of the Great Witley estate to pay the debts.

It was bought by the trustees of William Humble Ward, 10th Baron Ward of Birmingham, for £890,000. His son, who was created Earl of Dudley, was one of the richest men in England, with a huge industrial fortune derived from the iron industry and coal mines around Dudley Castle in Staffordshire. In 1883, the Dudley estates comprised 4,730 acres in Staffordshire, and 14,698 acres in Worcestershire and bits elsewhere, totalling 25,554 acres and bringing in an annual income of £123,176. Much of this was lavished on Witley Court, which was transformed into a model Victorian estate with a palatial seat at its centre. The architect, Samuel Dawkes, enlarged and remodelled the house, encasing it in ashlar stone in the 1850s. William Andrews Nesfield was employed to lay out colourful parterres and formalise the gardens in 1854. Nesfield referred to this lavish job as his 'monster' work. The *pièce de résistance* was the Perseus and Andromeda Fountain, with carved statues by Forsyth on a plinth 26 feet high, and the hardly less enormous Flora Fountain. Perseus made a 'noise like an express train' when it was fired and could

♔ *The entrance front and chapel in 1897.*

B Looking through the columns of the portico over the park with Repton's landscaping and additional Victorian planting including magnificent Wellingtonias. Much of the woodland was felled when the estate was sold in 1938–39, individual woods being sold separately for their timber.

P Looking over the Perseus Pond to the Golden Gates before their sale and removal.

entertainment venue. (Dudley Castle itself was sold in 1937, and rather improbably, became a zoo with good modern buildings.)

At Great Witley, the outlying farms were sold after the First World War and the nucleus of the estate, including the house and park, purchased in 1920 by Sir Herbert Smith (d. 1943), a carpet manufacturer from Kidderminster, who received a Lloyd George baronetcy in the same year (ostensibly for services during wartime). He was a characteristic self-made 'millionaire' of the time, the owner of Carpet Trades Limited, and chairman of Castle Motors Limited in Kidderminster. Sir Herbert was not popular – indeed, his local nickname was 'Piggy'. He bought Great Witley, like his baronetcy, out of a sense of *folie de grandeur* and was unable to support the 'life style' it represented: he hardly lived there and tried to run it with a skeleton staff. Gradually, the place went downhill and the *coup de grâce* was a fire on 7 September 1937, which broke out in the servants' quarters and part-gutted the house. This provided the excuse for selling up and general asset-stripping.

A year later, on 26 September 1938, the estate of 1,000 acres was put up for sale, 'by direction of Sir Herbert Smith, Bt. In consequence of a Fire which has destroyed part of the mansion'. The sales particulars prepared by Jackson Stops expatiated on the 'wonderful grounds and Parklands', the Home Farm, 'with period house suitable for conversion into a Gentleman's House, Deer Park House, The Gardener's House, and Enclosed Gardens'. Attention was drawn to the picturesque landscape of the estate, with the 600-feet high Woodbury Hill. The main emphasis, however, was on the 'magnificent timber' in the woodlands. This included 617,915 'cubic feet of mature oak' and was sold in 53 lots to timber merchants for felling. The Wilderness divided into three lots brought £7,865, the Lodge Plantations (lots 6, 7 and 8) brought in £5,500 and the Deerbarn Covert £18,000.

The architectural components, such as gates, statues, balustrades, carved marble lions and much else, were not so easy to sell despite an optimistic assurance that 'Corporations, Architects and builders will find plenty here to enrich their towns, parks and buildings'. The lush description of the 1st Earl of Dudley's architectural embellishments concluded with a desperate plea to Midlands businessmen: 'How could a man do better than present to his birthplace one of these works of art?' Some carved stone work did make its way to the war memorial

⚘ The Golden Gates were sold in 1938. This photograph was published by Country Life *in 1897.*

garden in Stourport, but otherwise the auctioneers and Sir Herbert were left with the bulk of Great Witley still on their hands, including the two giant fountains.

A further sale (also by Jackson Stops) was held on 4 April 1939 at the Swan Hotel, Stourport. This was for the house, lodges and 587 acres. There was no hope of selling *en bloc*, so the remaining property was divided into eight lots. Again, the particulars drew attention to the 'Wonderful Grounds, Parkland and Lakes'. This time, however, attention was focussed on the proximity of Birmingham and the suitability of the place for building rich villas for commuters: 'Park and Lakeside Land providing Magnificent Sites for houses'. (Sir Herbert was getting desperate.) 'The estate which is to be sold offers unlimited possibilities to investors for development' and 'demolition contractors'. This time Worcester Lodge fetched £500, the Stourport Lodge £450, The Red House £800, the lake and 13 acres overlooking it £700; frontage sites on the main road went for £450. The main house and gardens formed Lot 1 in the sale: 'If Lot 1 is not sold a Demolition Sale will be held of the Mansion House and Garden embellishments at a date to be announced later.'

But it did not sell and was acquired subsequently by W. Collington & Son, demolition contractors. However, the outbreak of the Second World War saved the shell of Witley Court and its magnificent fountains. There was no opportunity to sell the components, though the contractors wrote to Coventry City Council immediately after the disastrous German bombing raid of December 1940, which flattened the city centre, offering Witley and its architectural outworks and fountains for incorporation in the rebuilt city. Unsurprisingly, this disingenuous offer fell on deaf ears amid the still-smouldering débris of Coventry. The Ministry of Works then gloriously scheduled the now-roofless ruins as an Ancient Monument, which prevented further attempts at demolition. Historic Buildings listing subsequently strengthened the statutory protection. After the War in 1953, the site was bought for £20,000 by the Wigington family (who still own the freehold) and entered into a guardianship agreement with the Department of the Environment. This has enabled the programme of repair and restoration of the shell of the house and the gardens to proceed in phases, from the 1970s to the present day, though much remains to be done and many elements have been lost – including a park lodge in the deer park with an eighteenth-century portico, which was blown up during the War as part of the routine destruction of that era, where the 'home team' did more damage to English rural architecture than the Germans.

Great Witley is unique in the history of the English country estate, both for the golden opulence of its Victorian and Edwardian embellishment and social and architectural apogee, and also for the fact that some of it was eventually saved from total destruction by State intervention in the last resort. As an afterthought, it should perhaps be

The garden front before the fire. The sculptured lions have disappeared.

pointed out that the present, 4th Earl of Dudley bought Great Hundridge Manor, a charming brick, seventeenth-century house near Chesham in Buckinghamshire, after the Second World War and still lives there. Two large wings in the same style were added, more than doubling the size of the house, and a new stable block built in 1962 to the design of Trenwith Wills (a pupil of Detmar Blow). That is now the more modest Dudley family seat, far from the source of their wealth in the Black Country.

⚓ *The gutted shell which was saved by being taken into guardianship in 1972 by the Department of the Environment, and is now maintained as a stabilised ruin by English Heritage.*

⚓ *Garden Temple, sold in 1939. Much of the architectural detail in the grounds including stone balustrades and statuary was sold in bits after the fire.*

The chapel, orangery, winter garden, shell of the house and overgrown gardens, before the restoration of Nesfield's parterre and fountains by English Heritage.

Index

⚘ Picture credits ⚘

Getty Images: 1, 34, 35, 164 (top), 173 (top)

English Heritage/National Monuments Record: 2-3, 4-5, 8,
11, 12-13, 18-19, 20-21, 25, 27, 31, 40, 43 (bottom), 44, 45, 46-47,
48, 49, 50-51, 52-53, 54, 55, 56-57, 58-59, 60-61, 62 (bottom),
63 (top), 64-65, 66-67, 68-69, 70-71, 74, 75, 76, 77, 78, 79,
80, 81, 82, 88, 91, 92, 95, 96, 98, 99, 100 (left), 102 (bottom),
106-107, 108, 110, 111, 112, 113, 114, 115, 122, 123, 124-125, 126-127,
128-129, 130, 131, 132, 133, 134-135, 136, 137, 138-139, 140, 141, 143,
144, 148, 149, 150-151, 152, 154 (bottom), 155 (top), 157, 158,
159, 166 (bottom), 167 (top), 168 (top), 169 (top and left), 170
(bottom), 172, 174, 176-177,178-179, 180, 184, 185 (bottom),
186, 187, 188, 189, 190, 191, 194-195, 196-197, 198-199, 200-201,
203, 204-205, back endpapers

Mary Evans Picture Library: 9, 41, 90

Derbyshire Local Studies Libraries and
www.picturethepast.org.uk: 102 (top)

Pilkington Group Ltd: 130, 133 (top), 136

Topfoto: 10

The Roger Mann Collection: 23, 171, 173 (bottom)

Imperial War Museum Archives: 32, 33

Alamy: 38, 39, 72, 73, 93

Country Life Picture Library: front endpapers, 43 (top),
84-85, 86-87, 116, 117, 118, 119, 120, 121, 142, 151 (bottom), 153,
154 (top), 156, 160-161, 162, 163, 164 (bottom), 165, 166 (top),
167 (bottom), 168 (bottom), 169 (bottom right), 170 (top),
181, 182, 183, 185 (top), 192, 202

Images from the Spanton Jarman Collection reproduced
by permission of Bury St Edmunds Past and Present
Society supplied by Suffolk Record Office: 94, 97, 101

Arundel Castle Archives: 22, 104, 105

Courtauld Institute of Art: 146-147

Nuttall Historical Society: 155 (bottom)